Pub 9.56

Twayne's United States Authors Series

EDITOR OF THIS VOLUME

Warren French

Indiana University

Robert Coover

TUSAS 400

Robert Coover

ROBERT COOVER

By RICHARD ANDERSEN

TWAYNE PUBLISHERS
A DIVISION OF G. K. HALL & CO., BOSTON

Copyright © 1981 by G. K. Hall & Co.

Published in 1981 by Twayne Publishers,
A Division of G. K. Hall & Co.
All Rights Reserved

Printed on permanent/durable acid-free paper and bound
in the United States of America.

First Printing

Library of Congress Cataloging in Publication Data

Andersen, Richard, 1946–
Robert Coover.

(Twayne's United States authors series ; TUSAS 400)
Bibliography: p. 149–54
Includes index.
1. Coover, Robert—Criticism and interpretation.
PS3553.O633Z53   813'.53   80-26365
ISBN 0-8057-7330-4

FOR: DEBORAH AND JACKIE

Contents

About the Author

Preface

Acknowledgments

Chronology

1. The Early Works 15

2. From Brunists to Baseball 40

3. More Exemplary Fictions 79

4. The Later Works 108

5. On Coover 141

 Notes and References 145

 Selected Bibliography 149

 Index 155

About the Author

Richard Andersen is a writer. He holds degrees from Loyola University of Los Angeles, Richmond College of the City University of New York, and New York University. In addition to articles published in professional journals and popular magazines, his book-length works include *William Goldman*, a critical study of the author's novels, *Straight Cut Ditch*, a novel about child abuse in education, *Muckaluck*, a fictional history of the Muckaluck Indian War of 1872, and *The World's Greatest Runner*, a fictional biography of Felix Carvajal, the world's greatest unknown marathoner.

Preface

ALTHOUGH A BIBLIOGRAPHY of Robert Coover's books is shorter than that of America's most important writers, few authors can match his range of styles and subject matter. Well before *The Public Burning* (1977) established his prominence in contemporary fiction, Coover had achieved a reputation for originality and versatility. His first book, *The Origin of the Brunists* (1966), a mostly naturalistic treatment of a mine disaster and the subsequent founding of a religious cult, proved his ability to handle traditional novel forms as well as ironically manipulate them into a parody of narrative conventions. A satire on the origins of Christianity, the book also dramatizes man's need to impose order on his world through fiction and the danger of believing in it as if it were truth. Coover explored further the relationship between man and the fictions he creates to order his world in his second novel, *The Universal Baseball Association, Inc., J. Henry Waugh, Prop.* (1968). To escape the drudgery of his life as an accountant, Henry Waugh invents a parlor baseball game with which he soon becomes obsessed. By the novel's end, Henry has disappeared into the fictions that the characters in his original fiction have created. In *Pricksongs and Descants* (1969), a collection of stories that are so diverse in subject and style they seem as if they might have been written by as many different authors, Coover examines the role of the fiction maker in an age when traditional narrative forms are no longer viable. Whether retelling from a new point of view such familiar stories as "Noah and the Ark" and "Little Red Riding Hood" or creating an entirely original work like "The Babysitter," in which virtually anything can/cannot and does/does not happen, Coover centers his self-reflexive focus on the writer, whose job it is to liberate his readers from inherited contents and conventions by challenging their traditional visions with fresh new ways of talking about the human experience. Perhaps to broaden his audience, Coover recast the central concerns of *Pricksongs and Descants* into four plays, which he collected under the title *A Theological Position* (1972). It was not until his treatment of Richard Nixon, Uncle

Sam, and the Rosenbergs appeared in *The Public Burning*, however, that the ideas and styles Coover began developing ten years before *The Origin of the Brunists* reached the popular readership.

The primary purpose of this book, then, is to analyze in detail the texts of Coover's works as they develop his ideas about the role of the fiction maker. This is the most appropriate theme for the first book on Coover's works for several reasons. It is the central concern of all his works and has been inadequately discussed by critics, who, more often than not, have commented upon Coover's works as individual pieces rather than as an oeuvre in which a single theme is developed. Furthermore, Coover's interest in the fiction maker's role serves as a metaphor from which to discuss the author's view of such significant issues as the transforming power of the imagination, man's need to order through fictions the chaos of his world, his tendency to believe as truth the fictions he has created, the stultifying effects of such dogmatic fictions as religion, history, science, and mathematics, and how these subjects reveal humanity's inner desire to self-destruct.

In order to facilitate a clear understanding of the development of Coover's treatment of the fiction maker's role, his works, for the most part, are treated chronologically. If there seems to be a sort of mechanical pattern developing in this chronology as the book evolves, the development is probably organic rather than managed since the role of the writer, in spite of the diverse range of subjects, is the common denominator of all Coover's works. Each chapter of the book, then, discusses a particular phase of Coover's central focus along with the secondary but equally important issues pertinent to the fictions discussed in that chapter. The presentation of the issues is enriched by excerpts from interviews that Frank Gado, Leo Hertzel, and Geoffrey Wolff conducted with Coover from 1968 to 1977. Parts of these interviews that are not referred to in the chapters pertaining to Coover's works provide this book's first chapter, in which Coover discusses the role of the fiction maker in general. In addition, references are made throughout the book to Coover's reviews and criticisms. Through these works, his plays, short stories, and novels, Coover creates a portrait of the issues confronting the people of the twentieth century and how they are responding to them.

RICHARD ANDERSEN

Acknowledgments

I WISH TO EXTEND a special note of gratitude to Jess Bessinger, this book's first critic, to Warren French, its most excellent editor, and to those whose works are the foundation upon which *Robert Coover* rests: Leo Hertzel, Robert Towers, William Gass, Frank Gado, Geoffrey Wolff, Margaret Heckard, Arlen Hansen, Jackson Cope, Neil Schmitz, Robert Scholes, Joyce Carol Oates, Jessie Gunn, Wilfred Sheed, Frank Shelton, Judith Wood Angelius, Linda Westervelt, Linda Mahin, and, most importantly, Larry McCaffery.

Others who contributed to the work and to whom I wish to acknowledge my appreciation are Robert Coover, Roni Natov, Stewart Tabakin, Bob Greene, Paul Levine and Janet Deegan.

Chronology

1932   Born February 4, Charles City, Iowa.

1953   Graduated from Indiana University with a Bachelor of Arts degree. Joined the Navy.

1960   "One Summer in Spain," *Fiddlehead.*

1961   "Blackdamp," *Noble Savage.*

1962   "The Square Shooter and the Saint," *Evergreen Review* 25. "Dinner with the King of England," *Evergreen Review* 27.

1963   "The Second Son," *Evergreen Review* 31.

1965   "The Neighbors," *Argosy* (London), January. Marries Maria del Pilar Sans Mallafre on June 3. The Coovers have three children: Diana Nin, Sara Chapin, and Roderick Luis.

1966   *The Origin of the Brunists.* Teaches at Bard College in New York.

1967   Teaches at the University of Iowa. "D.D., Baby," *Cavalier* (July). "The Mex Would Arrive in Gentry's Junction at 12:10," *Evergreen Review* 47.

1968   Writer in Residence at Wisconsin State University. *The Universal Baseball Association, Inc., J. Henry Waugh, Prop.* "The Cat in the Hat for President," *New American Review* 4.

1969   Rockefeller Foundation Fellowship. Writer in Residence at Washington University in St. Louis. *Pricksongs and Descants.* "Letter from Patmos," *Quarterly Review of Literature. On a Confrontation in Iowa City,* a film written, directed, and produced by Coover.

1970   "The Last Quixote," *New American Review* 11. "The Reunion," *Iowa Review.* "Some Notes on Puff," *Iowa Review.*

1971   Guggenheim Fellowship. "The First Annual Congress of the High Church of Hard Core (Notes from the Underground)," *Evergreen Review* 89. "McDuff on the Mound,"

Iowa Review. "Encounter" and "Debris," *Panache.* Citation in fiction from Brandeis University.

1972   Teaches at Princeton University. *A Theological Position* (plays). *The Water-Pourer.* "Beginnings," *Harper's.* "Lucky Pierre and the Music Lesson," *New American Review* 14.

1973   Teaches at Vanderbilt Military Institute. "The Dead Queen," *Quarterly Review of Literature.*

1974   Guggenheim Fellowship. "The Public Burning of Ethel and Julius Rosenberg: An Historical Romance," *TriQuarterly* 26, later expanded into *The Public Burning* (1977). "Lucky Pierre and the Cunt Auction," *Antaeus.*

1975   "Whatever Happened to Gloomy Gus of the Chicago Bears?" *New American Review.* "Lucky Pierre and the Coldwater Flat," *Penthouse.*

1976   "The Fallguy's Faith," *TriQuarterly.*

1977   *The Public Burning.* "The Tinkerer," Antaeus. "The Master's Voice," *New American Review.* "The Convention," *Panache.*

1979   "In Bed One Night," *Playboy.*

CHAPTER 1

The Early Works

I "Exemplary Fictions"

IN 1613, with one foot already in the stirrup, Miguel de Cervantes Saavedra wrote in his prologue to "Two Exemplary Fictions" that "his intention has been to set up in the public square of our country a billiard table where everyone may come to amuse himself without harm to body or soul; for decent and pleasing pastimes are profitable rather than harmful. One is not always in church or engaged in prayer; one is not always occupied with business matters, however important they may be. There is a time for recreation, when the tired mind seeks repose."[1]

In his prologue to "Seven Exemplary Fictions," which he dedicates to Cervantes, Robert Coover celebrates his exemplar's endorsement of fiction as a form of recreation. In fact, Coover's collection of short works has often been described as if they were games: "Most of the fictions in Robert Coover's remarkable new volume are solitaires—sparkling, many-faceted. Sharply drawn and brightly painted paragraphs are arranged like pasteboards in ascending or descending scales of alternating colors to compose the story, and the impression that we might scoop them all up and reshuffle, altering not the elements but the order or the rules of play, is deliberate."[2]

Referring to his and Cervantes's mutual friend, "don Roberto S.," the author of *The Fabulators*, Coover emphasizes his interest in providing his readers with the kinds of literary games that are necessary for a healthy imagination. Scholes explains that modern fabulators, such as Coover, John Barth, Kurt Vonnegut, and Iris Murdoch, "tend to be more playful and more artful in construction"[3] than their literary predecessors. The result is a wide-ranging set of narrative forms that invite readers to relinquish some of their conventional approaches to literature and participate with their authors in games of wit that more often than not juxtapose the fantastic in life with the everyday. In an essay entitled, "The Last Quixote: Marginal Notes on the Gospel According to Samuel Beckett," Coover recognizes his indebtedness to the master absurdist and introduces to literature a name for these specialized readers capable of enjoying the puzzles, riddles, and verbal games of their authors' preoccupation. He calls them "initiates."

Nevertheless, there is more to this new expression of fiction than playing games. In the same way that Cervantes's exemplary stories also represent the different writing ideas and human truths with which their author worked since about 1580, so too does "Seven Exemplary Fictions" represent all of Coover's concerns from 1957, when he first began writing, to 1962, when he commenced his first novel. In the prologue to these early works, which include three fictions collected under the title "The Sentient Lens," Coover praises Cervantes for having the courage to turn away from his age's worn-out ideologies and overused literary convention, the Romance, and focus instead on new ways of telling good stories and telling them well. Crediting Cervantes with having given birth to the novel, Coover sees the *maestro*'s fictional innovations as a part of a discovery process that is vital if man expects to consistently create relevant ways of describing his condition.

Unfortunately, says Coover, most of today's writers have lost their desire for the thrill of discovery. Content with the familiar and having their already held viewpoints about the world confirmed, they have eaten away at the aura of open-ended optimism created by Cervantes's narrative revolution and ended up in a blind alley of exhausted forms and ideas. Consequently, Coover exhorts his literary contemporaries to challenge themselves by challenging the assumptions of their inherited age and sally forth toward new worlds of fiction. Never mind that the only vehicle available is a pile of bones, he says; use the familiar and worn out to combat the content of hackneyed forms and "to conduct the reader to the real, away from mystification to clarification, away from magic to maturity, away from mystery to revelation" (*PD*, p. 78).[4] Barber's basin on his head, Coover leads his initiates beyond structural games to the less frequently seen side of props and mirrors as he attempts to make clear rather than merely present illusion. Giving forms to his materials that resist being reduced to a formula, Coover offers his readers indispensable funds of information and ideas about fiction-making and human nature.

Because Coover's short fictions study the process of their narration as they proceed, they have been categorized as "metafiction" by both Robert Scholes and Neil Schmitz.[5] As with the works of writers such as Thomas Pynchon, John Barth, Vladimir Nabokov, and J. L. Borges, Coover's stories are what Roger Shattuck has referred to as "self-reflexive" literature, that is, they insist on being recognized as their own artistic subjects.[6] To make the reader constantly aware that what he is reading is an art form that is equally as important as its author's comment on the human condition, Coover creates elaborate artifices into which he places his characters and their events. Because these characters and actions tend to be types drawn from the popular culture, however, they enrich rather than balance the artifacts Coover has imagined. Furthermore, these familiar personae create in the readers' mind stereotypical responses that the author manipulates by sending them in unexplored directions.

Coover's attempts in "Seven Exemplary Fictions" and "The Sentient Lens" to shock his readers out of their conventional approaches to literature fall into two categories. The first category involves the reinterpretation of stories that have been accepted uncritically for ages. By providing these stories with alternative perspectives, Coover hopes to free his readers from some of the cultural clichés they have unconsciously assimilated. "Our old faith—one might better say our old sense of constructs derived from myths, legends, philosophies, fairy stories, and other fictions which help to explain what happens to us from day to day, why our governments are the way they are, why our institutions have the character they have, why the world turns as it does—has lost its efficacy. Not necessarily is it false; it is just not as efficacious as it was" (Gado, pp. 143–44). The second category into which the remainder of Coover's exemplary fictions may be placed concerns stories that present fiction as a variety of narrative possibilities. These stories are designed to subvert their readers' accepted literary conventions and simplistic ideas about human nature and help them recognize and attain higher levels of artistic consciousness. "Most of society's effort goes into forging the construct, the creative form in which everybody can live—a social contract of sorts. . . . Whatever form they set up is necessarily entropic; eventually it runs down and is unable to propel itself past a certain point. When it does that it becomes necessary to do everything that has been taboo: wear women's clothes, kill the sacred animal and eat it, screw your mother, etc. A big blast reduces everything to rubble; then something new is built. . . . Artists recreate; they make us think about doing all the things we shouldn't do, all the impossible apocolyptic things, and weaken and tear down structures so that they can be rebuilt, releasing new energies" (Gado, p. 157).

Coover's principal method for liberating his readers from sensibilities that have been deadened by the familiar is irony. Speaking of himself and other contemporary writers whose tendency was once to reject traditional narrative forms, Coover says, "We are turning back to design and there is an attraction towards modes of inquiry and creation that we rejected as we moved into this Era of Enlightenment. Those forms . . . have a certain beauty, and now a potential for irony exists in them. . . . They *are* useful" (Gado, p. 143). Irony enables Coover and his readers to distance themselves from traditional narrative forms without isolating themselves from the human content of those forms. Consequently, Coover's readers are able to enjoy their author's poking fun at literature's inherited conventions without losing their concern for humanity's condition. The result is a healthy sense of humor and the awareness of a changing consciousness.

Of the "Seven Exemplary Fictions," "The Brother" and "J's Marriage" serve as models for the reinterpretation of Bible stories. Coover explains the creative genesis of these fictions as well as the retelling of another Bible story, "The Reunion": "Like a lot of young undergraduates, I had been attracted to courses in theology and the philosophy of religion. The problem of Christian belief bothered me: it wouldn't leave me alone and yet I couldn't solve it. Then I found a vibrant way to understand the matter: I imagined a character like Jesus, created him in my own mind, and carried this thing on with him. Rather than try to discuss the historical arguments for his existence or non-existence, or to investigate what had happened to the Gospel texts and how much we could depend on the various parts, I merely took the story itself and, involving myself in it, considered various variations.

"At about that time, I encountered an argument between a theologian named Rudolf Bultmann and a philosopher named Karl Jaspers. Bultmann, a dogmatist, felt that the church was reeling under the attack of the Enlightenment. (He was discovering this a little late—three hundred years after—but never mind.) He believed that Christianity ought to de-mythologize itself. Out should go the Noah story, Adam and Eve, the Virgin Birth, all those things that looked ridiculous to the modern eye—but not the Resurrection. The Resurrection had to be saved because it was that moment in which God's finger touched history. . . . Jaspers got into an argument with him, and it was this subsequently published correspondence that I was reading. For Jaspers, the argument was obvious: if you throw the rest out, you've got to throw the Resurrection out too. But, why throw any of it? Why not accept it all as story; not as literal truth but simply as a story that tells us something, metaphorically, about ourselves and the world? Jaspers concluded that the only way to struggle against myth is on myth's own ground.

"When I read that . . . I found in Jasper's coherent statement a verification of what I had been writing clumsy notes to myself about. How liberating that recognition was! I went on to write "The Reunion," a story about Thomas explaining to the other disciples why the hanged man they are waiting for won't come—and then, of course, after he's done a good job of this, the man does come, much to everybody's astonishment. (It was supposed to be in *Pricksongs*, but it had been put away in a folder for so long that I forgot it when I turned in the manuscript)" (Gado, pp. 153–54).

"The Brother" retells the story of Noah from the perspective of Noah's brother, a victim of the flood that covered the earth for forty days and nights. Told in the stream-of-consciousness, modern-sounding voice of the brother, the story provides its readers with a human intimacy that quickly wins their affection for the people doomed by God's arbitrary wrath. Preventing the story from being reduced to pathos, however, is the humor and genuine love that exists between Noah's brother and his wife. Joking over a bottle of wine about the number of animals Noah is cramming into the ark, the brother says,

. . ."All kindsa damn animals and birds and things I ain't never seen the likes" and my wife says . . . "I bet he ain't got no lice" and we both laugh like crazy and when I can says "oh yes he does less he's took a bath" and we both laugh till we're cryin and we finish off the wine and my wife says "look now I *know* what he ain't got. He ain't got no termites" and I says "you're right I don't recollect no termites maybe we oughta make him a present" and my wife holds me close quiet all of a sudden and says "he's really movin Nathaniel's really movin" and she puts my hand down on her round belly and the little fella is kicken up a terrific storm and I says kinda anxious "does it hurt? do you think that—?" and "no" she says "it's good" . . . and we drain what's left in the bottom of our cups and the next day we wake up in each other's arms and it's rainin and *thank God* we say. . . ." (*PD*, p. 96)

The humor and affection in this scene is made increasingly more poignant by the tension that exists between what is occurring in the story and what the reader knows is to come. This tension is increased by such ironic comments as the brother's italicized "*thank God.*"

Because they are farmers, Noah's brother and his wife are happy when the rains first arrive. The downpour also provides them with the opportunity to stay inside, enjoy each other's company, and do things around the house. What begins as joy, however, soon turns to terror. The rain does not stop. The crops are destroyed. The farm animals drown. Desperate to save his life and those of his wife and unborn child, the brother goes to Noah and asks him if he and his wife may board the ark until the storm blows over, but Noah ignores him. Frantically, the brother makes his way back to his house where he finds his wife drowned. He then climbs to the top of a hill that overlooks his farm to await the inevitable.

In "J's Marriage," Coover tells the Bible story of Mary's immaculate conception from her husband's point of view. Unlike "The Brother," which is presented in a manner usually associated with James Joyce, Coover's reinterpretation of the Mary and Joseph story is told by a third-person narrator who seems to have been significantly influenced by Henry James:

In fact, it wouldn't be unkind to say, and he brought himself to confess it in the torment of his most rational moments, that a good many of the most beautiful things he said to her she failed to understand, or rather, she understood not the sense of them, but merely the apparent emotion, the urgency, the adoration behind them. (*PD*, p. 112)

Nevertheless, while the introspective prose style is as appropriate for Joseph's reflective personality as is the immediate, impetuous one for Noah's brother, it is balanced by Kafkaesque references to Joseph as "J." In addition to providing another side to a familiar story, Coover may also be making a comment on the modern existential man of above-average intelligence who has a difficult time understanding his irrational world.

"J's Marriage" opens with a description of Joseph and Mary's courtship, (*PD*, 112), in which Joseph makes more than a few unrequited overtures of love. Eventually they wed, but their marriage is not consummated. Apparently, Mary loves and trusts Joseph enough to sleep beside him, but she cannot bring herself to make love with him. Joseph sees Mary's rejection as a sign that she does not really love him as much as she says, but he believes that if he is patient and understanding, his wife will, in time, return his affection and reward his self-denial. Ironically, the first time Mary can bring herself to appear naked before her husband, she tells him she is going to have God's baby.

Prone to be melancholy, Joseph suffers a breakdown from his inability to convince himself that God has not betrayed him. Though Joseph's health eventually improves, his relationship with Mary does not. After the Christchild is born, Joseph is able to consummate his marriage, but he has little enthusiasm for the act. His life with Mary is comfortable, even pleasant, but it lacks excitement and energy. The holy couple's marriage ends when Joseph dies ignobly of consumption.

In an article entitled "Robert Coover and the Hazards of Metafiction," Neil Schmitz credits Coover with having created skillful tricks of interpretation in "The Brother" and "J's Marriage," but once "the trick is grasped, all that remains is an irreligious jest on the order of Mark Twain's *Letters from the Earth*."[7] While it is true that when readers begin these stories they will not be immediately aware that the fictions are a reinterpretation, their recognition of Coover's "trick" certainly amounts to something more than a joke. As evidenced in the careful treatment given Noah's brother, his family, and Joseph, Coover is as much interested in the suffering of everyday people as he is in performing literary acrobatics. Because his readers are familiar with the principal characters of these stories, Coover can focus attention on those people who have been victimized by God's work. It *does* matter, he is saying, that unborn children, pregnant wives, and relatives who helped Noah build the ark are left to drown. It *does* matter that Joseph has been hurt and abused by the vulgar act for which God is responsible. The real issues for today's readers of the Bible stories and the new perspectives of them that Coover offers, then, are not the cosmic interpretations of the past, "because we don't believe in a Godhead any more and the sense of a purposeful unity has vanished" (Gado, p. 143), but rather an appreciation of events that can be understood and felt in human terms.

Coover further emphasizes the disparity that exists between myth and reality by juxtaposing his characters. In "The Brother" and "J's Marriage," Noah and Mary maintain the same relatively abstract personalities that they have in the Bible. Unemotional, humanly detached, compliant instruments of God's will, they appear vacuous when compared with the brother and Joseph, whose personal losses the reader appreciates much more acutely than he would were they merely caricatures in an "irreligious jest."

Though not one of Coover's "Seven Exemplary Fictions," "The Reunion"[8] deserves consideration here because it is a retelling of a familiar Bible story, namely, Christ's appearance before the apostles after his Resurrection. Unlike "The Brother" and "J's Marriage," however, this story does not remain faithful to the original. "The Reunion" begins with Doubting Thomas telling the apostles about how important it is to "confront reality honestly and bravely, one's own wishes be damned" (p. 64). Just as Thomas convinces Christ's followers that they have relied too heavily on the myth of the Messiah, however, Christ, who has been hanged rather than crucified, appears and accepts a chair offered to him by the doubting apostle. Unfortunately, Christ's head can no longer be supported by his broken neck and the physical effects of his hanging dominate the scene: "Again the head rolls off the man's shoulder, and now dangles over the back of the chair, staring upside down, at the circle of straight faces that stare. Thomas sees that the man cannot, by himself, return the head to the shoulder, but neither he nor anyone else in the room can bring himself to help the man. Instead he stares down at the stark and brittle body whose head has disappeared behind its back. The man in the chair does not move. Nor does he ever move again. It is a long and cheerless night" (p. 67).

For Coover, "The Reunion" is a pivotal work. It sacrifices the humor of "The Brother" and the bitter but human sensitiveness of "J's Marriage" for a more explicit delineation of the author's belief that his readers should consider Christian myths "not as literal truth but simply as story that tells us something metaphorically about ourselves and the world" (Gado, p. 154). By shifting the metaphor from Christ's redemption to mankind's overconfidence in myths,however, Coover opens up the possibility for different versions as well as different interpretations of traditional stories. A symbol for this idea may lie in the fact that none of Coover's three biblical retellings ends with a period, thereby suggesting that they can continue in a variety of ways. Furthermore, by rewriting, as opposed to retelling, the story of Christ's Resurrection, Coover exposes the undershaft of religious myths and provides his readers with an ironic commentary on how fictions, which have no more meaning than people assign to them, can be formulated into truths.

"Panel Game," "The Marker," "The Wayfarer," "In a Train Station," and "Klee Dead" continue to explore the possibilities of narration at the point where "The Brother," "J's Marriage," and "The Reunion" leave off in the sense that they emphasize the value of fiction without reducing it to the parodic reinterpretation of familiar stories. In these seemingly more modern tales, Coover also introduces his delight in games for their own sake as well as that of the reader, who, through them, is invited to contemplate the infinite possibilities of fiction and the human truths that exist within them. The *way* in which these stories are told, then, is not separate from but equal to *what* is being said. Technique and subject are not divided; they are one and the same in the various processes of narration that Coover explores.

The author's first invitation in "Seven Exemplary Fictions" for his readers to explore these unfamiliar narrative forms is "Panel Game," a television quiz show in which the contestant, "Unwilling Participant," who is also the reader, must guess the nature of the game being played. He is assisted but ultimately distracted by his fellow panelists, Aged Clown, Lovely Lady, and Mr. America.

Merry Moderator, who presides over the game, puts Unwilling Participant through a wringer of associations—"Back: Bach: Bacchus: baccate: berry. Raw berry? Strawberry? Maybe. Sticky berry in the raw? In the raw: bare. Bare berry: beriberi. Also bearberry, the dog rose, dogberry. Dogberry: the constable, yes, right, the constable in . . . what? *Comedy of Errors*! Yes. No"

(*PD*, p. 80)—but the outcome of the game is as inevitable as the coming of the rains in "The Brother." Unwilling Participant loses the game, the correct answer to which is *Much Ado About Nothing*, and, in the process, loses his life.

As much as the well-worn clichés of Bible stories have deadened the sensibilities of the contemporary consciousness, they have not been nearly as effective as the popular culture. Whereas religious myths once offered a sense of purpose and unity to the world and fulfilled a human need for a deity, quiz shows, Hollywood movies, spectator sports, television, pop novels, fast foods, and the like have been artificially created to satisfy the need for profit and to keep people from understanding what is happening to them. Popular culture, Coover is saying, is another word for mind control.

The people who view "Panel Game" live from the studio or on their television sets at home have seen the show and others like it played before. No longer sensitive to the real values of life, they look to the popular culture to provide for them experiences they have been convinced are authentic. Their values reinforced by the merry moderators of fashion, they then create culture heroes, such as Aged Clown, Lovely Lady, and Mr. America, to worship. These culture heroes, who embody mass ideals, confirm their disciples' addiction to participating in activities that protect them from what Plato has referred to as the pain of perception. Those who, like Unwilling Participant, do not wish to be a part of a fad, are labeled "Bad Sports" and summarily executed.

In addition to demonstrating the consciousness-crippling effects of popular culture, Coover introduces to literature the role of the reader as an active participant in the fiction he is reading:

You squirm, viced by Lady (who excites you) and America (who does not, but bless him all the same), but your squirms are misread: Lovely Lady lifts lashes, crosses eyes, and draws breath excitedly through puckered mouth as though sucking milkshakes through a straw, and, seemingly at the other end of the straw, the Moderator ingests: "Tsk, tsk!" and, gently reproving, waggles his dewlap. Audience howls happily the while and who can blame them? You, Sport, resign yourself to pass the test in peace and salute them with a timid smile, squirm no more. (*PD*, p. 80)

By entering the minds of his readers as well as those of his characters, Coover allows them to create themselves as they react to the events in which they are participating. In fact, the reactions of the reader, character, narrator, and author to the experiences described by Coover may provide a basic metaphor for his theory about the expansion of consciousness through the infinite possibilities of artistic forms.

Coover presents a parable of one of his artistic theories in "The Marker," the story of a young man named Jason, who, while reading a book, is called to make love by his beautiful wife. Jason places a marker in the book, puts the book on an end table, turns out the light by which he has been reading, and makes his way in the dark toward his wife's bed. The bed, however, is not where it was when the lights were on. Disoriented, Jason bumps into furniture and stumbles around the room until he finds himself back where he began. With his wife's laughter as guide, the young man eventually finds the bed. Suddenly, the lights come on and the lovers are interrupted by a police officer and his four assistants. When Jason discovers that he has been making love not with his beautiful wife but with a decomposing corpse, he is horrified.

The lovers in this parable are, as Larry McCaffery has suggested,[9] allegorical. Jason represents every reader whose vision has been limited by an adherence to traditional artistic forms. Like Jason's wife, these forms were once beautiful, but they are now dead and decaying. Rigor mortis has set in with them and is keeping readers like Jason from expanding his literary consciousness. The young man's aesthetic sterility is symbolized by his penis, which he has a difficult time removing from the corpse and which, when the police officer gets through with it, is no longer potent. Readers who reject alternative possibilities are making love to dead corpses, says Coover, who, through the police officer, clarifies this theory: "'You understand, of course,'" he says,

that I am not, in the strictest sense, a traditionalist. I mean to say that I do not recognize tradition *qua* tradition as sanctified in its own sake. On the other hand, I do not join hands with those who find inherent in tradition some malignant evil, and who therefore deem it of terrible necessity that all customs be rooted out at all costs. I am personally convinced, if you will permit me, that there is a middle road, whereon we recognize that innovations find their best soil in traditions, which are justified in their own turn by the innovations which crated them. I believe, then, that law and custom are essential, but that it is one's task to review and revise them. In spite of that, however, *some things still make me puke!* . . . *Now get rid of that fucking corpse.* (*PD*, p. 91)

While "The Marker" encourages readers to pull away from the deadening influences of tradition, "The Wayfarer," like "Panel Game," demonstrates the consequences rendered to those who choose to live outside of life's mainstream. Lonely, but secure in the knowledge that they are their own persons and not products of the popular culture, wayfarers have no need to respond to stimuli that alienate them from their authentic selves. Because wayfarers are a threat to the norm, however, society wants them eliminated. Speaking in another context, William Gass explains: "It is the principal function of the popular culture—though hardly its avowed purpose—to keep men from understanding what is happening to them, for social unrest would surely follow, and who knows what outbursts of revenge and rage."[10]

Even though the road to individuality may lead to physical death, however, it also leads to life. With the wayfarer as their exemplar, Coover wants his readers to deny the attractively packaged creeds of contemporary society with its superficial conception of life's possibilities, its dismissal of the genuine creative capacities of man, and its fear and dislike of any but the mildest and most familiar truths. By refusing to keep step with the popular culture's beat, the wayfarer denies his interest in the social order and any claim it thinks it may have on him.

Equally as important as the wayfarer in this tale is the narrator, who tries to persuade the "unsympathetic figure," sitting on a symbolic milestone, to join the bandwagon of popular thought. When the wayfarer recognizes his presence but refuses to respond to him, the narrator interprets the old man's silence as a form of arrogance. The wayfarer, on the other hand, sees no reason why he should have to justify his denial to the narrator. His refusal to participate needs no reasonable substantiation because it is a matter of taste and has reference to nothing but the nature of the wayfarer.

Frustrated by the wayfarer's refusal to communicate, the narrator, whose job is to keep people in line, tries to provoke the old man into speaking. The narrator stares at the wayfarer, bares his teeth at him, points his gun at him, punches it into his chest and groin, fires a shot over his head, breaks the old man's nose with the rifle butt, and, finally, puts a bullet through his chest. The wayfarer does not die easily, however, and the narrator has to shoot him in the head. Nevertheless, these atrocities do not prevent the narrator from being a sympathetic character. Recognizing that part of the wayfarer that lies deep within himself, the narrator cannot easily perform his duty and afterwards has a difficult time freeing the old man from his mind. Unfortunately, the narrator's guilt does not last long:

I watched the traffic. Gradually, I became absorbed in it. Uniformly it flowed, quietly, possessed of its own unbroken grace and precision. There was variety in detail, but the stream itself was one. One. The thought warmed me. It flowed away and away and the unpleasant images that had troubled my mind flowed away with it. At last, I sat up, started the motor, and entered the flow itself. I felt calm and happy. A participant. (*PD*, p. 124)

Unlike the narrator, who moves with the flow of his culture's traffic and is consequently isolated from himself, the wayfarer alienates himself from what is fashionable in the interest of his own freedom. In the degrees to which the wayfarer withdraws from society, he is less and less alienated from his authentic self. The more freedom he attains, the less can he be compelled to conform. The more he acts on behalf of his will, the more alienated he realizes he will become if he acts at the behest of another's will. In short, the less he expresses an externalized life, the more the wayfarer is able to realize his own life.

Having withdrawn from one social activity after another, the wayfarer seems to be almost comatose when the narrator approaches him. In allowing the narrator to shoot him, however, the wanderer reveals an unconscious desire to destroy not himself but those sensibilities of the narrator that are still incorporated into his psychic fabric and which are dangerous to the preservation of his inner self. The wayfarer, then, by allowing himself to be annihilated, annihilates the social order that exists within him.

Through "In a Train Station," Coover demonstrates a degree of freedom that fiction can attain when emancipated from the flow of a culture's literary traffic. At 9:27, Alfred purchases a

ticket for the 10:18 Express Train to Winchester, but the reader
is told that neither Alfred nor the train may be real. Nevertheless, Alfred engages in familiar conversation with the stationmaster. Beneath the surface of their conversation, however,
there is a tension that reveals an undefined control that the
stationmaster has over Alfred. The men's conversation is
interrupted by a derelict. Alfred, with quick glances at the
stationmaster, watches the drunk, who stumbles incoherently
around the train station. At one point, Alfred breaks the drunken
man's fall but is admonished by the stationmaster for having done
so. Alfred brushes aside the tears the stationmaster's words have
brought to his eyes, takes a knife out of a bag he is carrying, and
grasps the drunk by his hair. The stationmaster then takes the
knife and severs the fallen man's head. Alfred weeps while the
stationmaster carries the severed head into his office and the
train to Winchester pulls into the station. When the stationmaster returns, Alfred, who by now has missed his train, is still
crying. Shaking his head, the stationmaster resets the station's
clock to 9:26 and returns to his office. Alfred shudders, picks up
his bag, and walks to the ticket window. Presumably but not
necessarily, he will buy a ticket for the 10:18 Express Train to
Winchester.

By reminding him that the events of "In a Train Station" are
not real, Coover makes the reader as well as himself constantly
aware that anything contained in the story is not only possible
but justifiable. Unlike real events, what happens in fiction does
not have to be judged in terms of its relation to the world.
Fictional events can be enjoyed in terms of the conventions they
establish within the individual frameworks that have been
created for them. Having expanded his reader's consciousness to
be aware of the narrative process as he reads, however, Coover
reminds him through his repetition of the story's opening events
just how stifling is the effect of innovations that become
conventions. Were Coover's readers to encounter only narrative
forms similar to that of "In a Train Station," the effect might well
be like reading the same story over and over again. As a result,
they might find themselves weeping and shuddering as Alfred
does as he is forced to repeat continually the events of his story.

"Klee Dead," which could be subtitled "Expectations
Denied," is like Coover's other exemplary fictions in that it
destroys the conventional attitudes with which the reader can

approach literature. As with "In a Train Station," "Klee Dead" begins at an end or at least what seems to be an end: "Klee, Wilbur Klee, dies. Is dead, rather. I know I know: too soon. It should come, after a package of hopefully ingenuous preparations, at the end" (*PD*, p. 104). Having been told the outcome of the story, the reader expects to learn about Klee and the events that led up to his death. This, however, is only the first of several expectations that the narrator frustrates as he shifts fictional gears and begins a tale about old Millicent Gee. Don't get frustrated, Coover is saying to his readers. This story is artifice; it isn't real. Sit back and enjoy the ways I manipulate your expectations.

After relating how Millie lives with an old ram, some dead fish, and an assemblage of interfiliated cats, the narrator goes off on a tangent from which he has difficulty returning. Speaking of Millie's apartment and perhaps the art of writing as well, he says, "To be sure we seem impulsively driven to load up empty spaces, to plump some goddamn thing, any object, real, imagined, or otherwise, where now there might be happily nothing . . ." (*PD*, p. 106).

Suddenly after introducing Millie's son and then wishing he had not done so, Coover's perhaps too self-conscious narrator jumps back to Klee's story, announces the fact that Wilbur jumped from a high place, and then initiates a discussion on cause and effect. As for Klee, the narrator admits that he does not know who he is, nor does he care. Enough of Klee, he says, and calls for an assessment of the story up to this point. Before he can begin, however, the narrator initiates a story about Orval Nulin Evachefsky. At the point in this story where Orval jumps from a window and kills himself, the narrator returns to the story of Klee. A piece of paper near Klee's remains may or may not be a suicide note. Perhaps tired of the game of not satisfying his reader's expectations or maybe realizing that by this time the reader has understood what he is saying between the lines of the unrelated fictions, the narrator apologizes for wasting the fifteen minutes it took to read his story: "Even I had expected more. You are right to be angry" (*PD*, p. 111).

The least successful of the exemplary fictions, "Klee Dead" may perhaps have been too heavily influenced by Samuel Beckett's *Malone*, the narrator of which is similar to Coover's in that he is apologetic, preoccupied with seemingly insignificant details, and distracted by his analysis of the story he is telling. Furthermore, though Coover makes his point about the infinite possibilities of fiction, his technique for doing so is tediously obvious and lacks the insight into human nature that his other stories contain. Nevertheless, the apprentice writer succeeds in fighting his way clear of dead forms and deadening language. He has yet to chronicle the articulation of consciousness that Beckett achieves in his trilogy, but he is familiar with a good part of the territory paved by his exemplar. Standing at the beginning of a new age for literature, Coover states his own goals in his estimation of his master's worth:

He is like those great sculptors who spend whole lives in the restless pursuit of some impossible quality, a glance, a gesture, a pygmalion, a leg, who end up giving us not so much objects, as a process, humbling archetypal, preceptive—for whatever else Beckett's art is, it is a lifelong parable on what writing itself is all about, not so much a new narrative genre or rhetorical fashion . . . as a kind of eightfold path for the maker . . . on his way to failure, or exemplary settling down into the self through all the pseudo-selves and posturings, disguises, imaginative displacements, and with no illusions, doubting even the wherewithal.[11]

II   *"The Sentient Lens"*

Until recently, writers assumed that in addition to providing pleasure, the purpose of literature was to present realistic pictures of life for the edification of its readers. Today, many writers have come to believe that reality cannot be recorded, particularly contemporary reality, which does a good job at humbling the best any single imagination can produce. That it cannot be recorded does not mean, however, that versions of reality cannot be created and, though distinct from the actual, related to it in various ways. In order to construct fictions of this sort, writers such as Coover, Pynchon, and Barth have overruled the laws of nature as they have previously operated in literature in order to promote and give more power to the laws of narration, which, ideally, adhere to no precepts. These new constructs may be distinct from reality, but they are not separate entities unto themselves. Created by imaginations that have been formed by reality, the fictions of contemporary writers offer their readers a world that might at first glance seem unfamiliar but nevertheless can make a significant contribution to their understanding of the human condition.

Through the sketches that are collected under the title "The Sentient Lens," Coover, as he did in "Seven Exemplary Fictions," expands the narrative possibilities of fiction as a process. Like Beckett, however, he is not so much concerned with creating a variety of genres or styles as with pointing out the fallacies of conventional approaches to literature and exploring alternatives to already existing forms of narration. At the same time, Coover's explorations into the versions of reality he constructs provide a comment on human nature.

As the title of this collection of stories suggests, "Scene for 'Winter,'" "The Milkmaid of Samaniego," and "The Leper's Helix" are replies to those who believe that art is capable of producing a realistic picture of life. Even a narrative that is told through the eyes of a mechanical instrument cannot be objective. Because it must be manipulated by human hands, the art a lens produces is, by nature, sentient, that is, it is tarnished by the senses and emotions of the person operating the camera. Hence, no camera can remain neutral as long as its operator is responding to the scene he is observing. The pictures that are developed from cameras, then, are not records of reality, but rather versions of life that have been constructed by the photographer.

"Scene for 'Winter'" is a picture of "Winter" as viewed through the sentient lens of a movie camera. It is not long, however, before the person behind the lens begins responding to that which the camera cannot sense: sound. The camera focuses in the direction of the sound. As he did in "Klee Dead," the narrator interrupts his story to tell his readers how they are to respond—"We hesitate, expectant, straining to hear it again" (*PD*, p. 169)—but he does not satisfy the reader's expectations. Instead the narrator focuses his lens in the direction of another sound and discovers a white rabbit being stalked by a hunting dog. Forgetting about the animals, the man behind the camera aimlessly pans his surroundings. The reader disscovers he is in a park rather than a forest, as he was led to believe. Eventually a sleigh passes by the camera on a road that runs through the park. A man, who is following the sleigh, approaches. Again, the narrator makes sure the reader is aware of Coover's emphasis on

the story's artificial nature by interrupting his fiction to tell the
reader how he is to respond to the events he is witnessing. He
also reminds the reader of the camera's static. Continually
reminded that "Scene for 'Winter' " is an artifact, the reader is
conscious of the alternatives that reality denies. Hence he is not
much surprised when the narrator turns the man who has been
following the sleigh into a clown and then into the white rabbit
with a dog in in its mouth.

In a poem entitled "Barcelona Air Terminal, 28 May," which is
not a part of "The Sentient Lens" collection, Coover presents a
picture of winter in the process of dying.

> disguised in splintered warehouse shacks with
> cracks in less than all the windows;
> the wind does customary things with
> strings, with bits of paper scraps and
> wrappings ripped from cigarettes, and
> frets with a pile of usual ashes,
> washes the images out of my mind.
> . . . Worried doors,
> bored with motion, open to a last
> gust of departures and, sighing, close like
> rows of dying martyrs to the night. A
> flight of stairs: I mount, unmount them,
> count them, trace the lamplight where a
> barrel slumps, damp and musty,
> just the empty casing, lonely,
> only that barrel, disintegrating,
>
> waiting.[12]

"The Milkmaid of Samaniego," like "Scene for 'Winter' " and
"Barcelona Air Terminal, 28 May," offers Coover's readers an
example of the subjective nature of literature, but it also
examines through the camera's lens some of the stifling ways in
which conventional approaches to literature can dominate the
perception of narrative reality. The story opens with a country
scene that is so conventional the reader is aware of a milkmaid's
presence even though she has yet to appear:

We are, then, aware of her undeniable approach, . . . aware of her
pitcher, her starched white blouse and brightly flowered skirt, her firm
yet jubilant stride down the dusty road . . . leading to the arched

bridge, past the oaks and crypresses, twisted wooden fences, the haphazard system of sheep and cattle alongside the occasional cottage and frequent fields under the untempered ardor of summer sun. (*PD*, p. 175)

Because of his familiarity with traditional narrative forms, the reader can create scenes in his own mind before they actually appear in the story. The narrator explains that the conventions with which a reader approaches a story often act

almost as though there has been some sort of unspoken but well understood prologue, no mere epigraph of random design, but a precise structure of predetermined images, both basic and prior in us, that describes her to us before our senses have located her in the present combination of shapes and colors. (*PD*, p. 175)

When the milkmaid appears on the scene, she fits the description created by the reader's traditional responses to bucolic settings. As she approaches the arched bridge, the sentient lens is momentarily distracted and has to be refocused on the maid. Apparently the narrator of this story is not the cameraman but the director and is suspicious of anything that might disrupt the patterns predetermined by convention. When the scene shifts to a farmyard, another familiar element, a young man, appears. The lens focuses on the man's sexual qualities. The man and the maid exchange "charged glances," but the man's response shatters the pattern established by pastoral forms. Despite the plea of "No! not—!" from the director, who panics at the threat of a broken tradition, the man attacks the woman. The farmyard scene then dissolves quickly and the lens focuses instead on the original scene of the old man and the bridge, but this time the reader does not approach the scene with a set of predispositions. The woman is at first frightened by the unkempt wayfarer, but she eventually responds to his friendly overtures and accepts from him a few coins to compensate for the loss of her pitcher and its contents. The story ends with a dissolving shot of the pitcher, now broken into many pieces, some of which have fallen into the stream that flows beneath the arched bridge.

On one level "The Milkmaid of Samaniego" is a construct designed to make its readers aware of the limitations of conventional thinking and the narrow focus afforded by seemingly objective views of reality. On another level, the story is a parable about the advantages of accepting innovative forms of fiction. The milkmaid, who represents the reader who approaches each scene with assumptions derived from traditional artistic focuses, is shocked by the unexpected actions of the young man, who represents a possibility that does not exist in traditional bucolic romances. The camera represents the views of those who do not wish to see that which does not confirm their already held views of the world. Hence, the camera shifts its attention from the farmyard to the road by the bridge shortly after the young man begins his attack on the milkmaid. The empty pitcher, which symbolizes the reinforced familiar, which has to be protected, is now in fragments. Some of these pieces have been washed away by the stream, but those that remain can perhaps be reassembled into less restrictive, more meaningful artistic forms. Speaking about the conventions today's writers have inherited from the novel tradition, Coover suggests the advantage of revitalizing more ancient formulas: "I went through a period when I didn't want to read *anybody* in the novel tradition; I felt there had been no good English novelist since, roughly, before Defoe. I assumed that the stuff that is in a sense furthest in the past—that is the most dated, irrelevant, and useless to us—is what was published last year, and that fictions became more valuable, more relevant to us as they recede from us in time. To me, the pre-Cervantean stuff seemed the most important.

"I plunged into all the really ancient material, and I'm grateful to the bias I had which led me to it. Before I had developed this hypothesis, I looked on those really old things more as mythic residue than as real fiction, but when I went back to them, I suddenly found extraordinary imaginations at work. I approached them as I would approach my own stories, and I recognized that whether it was one guy or a bunch of people writing these things, here were intelligent approaches to fictional problems. Imagine how exciting, even unsettling, it was to make this discovery. . . .

"Needless to say, I've since backed away from that theory; I now seek my enthusiasms from the whole range of fiction. But it was a healthy attitude to hold for a time: I learned a lot and it has had a substantial influence on me" (Gado, pp. 146-47).

In "The Leper's Helix," Coover carries one step further his attempts to upset his readers' habitual perceptions of literature by introducing the most blatantly artificial narrative he has yet to create and then placing within that construct the nightmare reality of the grotesque. The story opens with the lens's vision of a leper approaching it on a circular path that at this point runs along the opposite side of an imaginary cone that has been formed by the movement of the camera. Because the speed with which the camera moves along its helix decreases as it progresses, the leper will eventually catch up with the narrator/cameraman and reader. Through the lens the reader sees increasingly more detailed descriptions of the leper, who at first creates an attractive picture. As he comes closer to the camera, however, the picture of the leper becomes grotesque. When the leper finally meets the narrator and the reader, he "hurls himself into our arms, . . . his sticky cold flesh fastening to us, me, his black tongue licking my face, blind eyes, that whine! his odors choking us, we lie, I lie helpless under the sickening weight of his perishing flesh" (*PD*, p. 182). Soon the embrace is over, however. The leper dies, and the narrator asks, "What terrible game will *you* play with *us*? me" (*PD*, p. 182). The answer is not stated here, but the reader knows from the other "Sentient Lens" stories and the "Seven Exemplary Fictions" that the possibilities are infinite.

Speaking of the nightmare quality that exists in his fiction as well as in that of some other contemporary writers, Coover identifies his use of the grotesque with a reaction against the limits of realism: "For one thing, the notion of realism as just call girls and naturals and that has through three and a half centuries of use become a little bit worn out. And there's a . . . sense that we've got to go back and discover a new interest for fiction, new ideas about what story writing is all about. And as a result, people are going back and breaking down all the old rules about having to tell a story that relates and is historically possible. And so to begin with, there's a search for new principles, a search for a new kind of outlook about what writing is all about, about what fiction is, what it can best do. . . . A lot of times it has to make deep plunges into states of being that are not what we think of as a walk on a sunny day. . . . Another thing is that there's no doubt that we've been pushed in the modern world to a state of extremity. . . . And this being the case, writers who are trying to express what is our reality today find in reality a kind of nightmare quality. They find this acting out of old rituals doesn't seem to have any meaning to us. They see us as behaving as though history had some meaning when history shows all signs of coming to an end. They can find little real valid positive moral response to a situation in which their own deaths would be interpreted as meaningless. I think . . . the writer . . . reveals and tries to get inside what life is all about and show . . . this to himself as much as to his reader. And he ends up engaged today, in this time, in something that is a bit like a nightmare" (Hertzel, pp. 25-26).

Nevertheless, Coover pays a price for his various techniques of defamiliarization. Through images such as the leper's embrace of the narrator, Coover has shocked his readers into perceiving the limits of realism, but at the same time he has lost his readers' willingness to become emotionally involved in his narratives. In a variety of detached intellectual ways, Coover has created artifices that are entertaining, but their insights into the human condition lack feeling. Through his self-conscious narrator, the cause-oriented Coover has constructed human styles rather than personalities. In this sense, then, he has succeeded in creating a "form" that equals its "content," but, with the exception of "The Brother" and "J's Marriage," Coover's triumph in his early works is questionable. Though intellectually stimulating, they are not human.

III   *The Adventures of Donald Warren*

"The Square-Shooter and the Saint" and "Dinner with the King of England" are two immature pieces of fiction that Coover published before he began writing his first novel, *The Origin of the Brunists,* and later decided to exclude from his collection of short works, *Pricksongs and Descants.* Because they depart only slightly from traditional realist forms and focus on a theme that is closer to the mainstream of American literature, the two stories may well have been written prior to some of the stories in "Seven Exemplary Fictions." The major failing of "The Square-Shooter and the Saint" and "Dinner with the King of England" lies in the tone Coover adopts toward his adolescent protagonist, Donald Warren. Because Coover describes Donald from the superior point of view of an adult, the protagonist comes across to the reader as somewhat ridiculous. Stories about adolescence that are genuinely mature, such as *The Adventures of Huckleberry*

Finn and *Catcher in the Rye,* enter into the lives of their adolescents at first hand and describe them through the eyes of their protagonists.

"The Square-Shooter and the Saint," which is subtitled "A Story About Jerusalem," opens with Donald pushing his red baseball cap back on his head as he views the holy city from the Mount of Olives. He is soon joined there by a slick, hashish-chewing, unkempt hippie woman named Laramie Down. They become friends, and, on their walk into Jerusalem, Layme provides Donald with a running commentary on the kind of attitude he should have toward any kind of institution, namely, negative. In spite of her stringy hair, bad smell, boorish manners, violent disposition, and face stained with hashish juice, Donald falls in love with Laramie: "The coarse gunnysack she was wearing, he thought tenderly, was a beautiful veil for the sensitivity that was sheltered within"[13] Eventually the two adolescents wind up in a nightclub where they drink more than they can handle. Because a waiter does not respond to her crude demands for another drink, Laramie delivers a tirade on phoniness to everyone in the restaurant. Beaning the waiter with her empty whiskey glass, she runs out a nearby exit as the restaurant's employees belt, kick, and hurl Donald into the street.

Because of the style in which it is narrated as well as the peculiar events it describes, "Dinner with the King of England" reads very much as if it might be a dream. In this story Donald is on an American Express tour that has made arrangements for him to have dinner with the King of England and other royalty at the Royal Palace. Trying to make Donald comfortable is a cigar-smoking duchess. Nevertheless, Donald feels so out of place that he makes a fool of himself in front of the entire assemblage. He mistakes a statue for a real person, twists the nose of a real person who looks like a statue, steps on the hem of the duchess's dress, thinks the band is playing "My Country 'Tis of Thee," gets bitten by one of the king's hunting dogs, and discovers his dinner bid is for the following evening. Baseball cap in hand, Donald leaves the Royal Palace a sadder but doubtfully wiser young man.

"The Square-Shooter and the Saint" and "Dinner with the King of England" are *Bildungsromans,* that is, they attempt to iniitiate their protagonist into the world of adult values. As in most stories of initiation, Donald is innocent, but he is not commmpletely naive. He is not corrupted by evil, but he can sometimes recognize it in others. On the other hand, he fails to recognize how dangerous is his ignorance of adult values. Not realizing what is taking place at the bar in Jerusalem, he is beaten by the restaurant's employees; in England, his innocent but immature behavior embarrasses the duchess. Because he is naive, Donald fails to make any connection between his innocence and the pain it inflicts.

Although Donald is a danger to himself and to others, he also embodies the one cohesive principle, love, which most lends itself to the preservation of life. That Donald can be both a destroyer and preserver is characteristic of his adolescence, a period of embodied contradictions. Because of the nature of this contradiction, Donald may at first seem as if he represents the confusions of the contemporary age or those of the New World in the Old. He does not. He is only an adolescent and not a very attractive one at that. His experiences and perspectives in Jerusalem and the Royal Palace enable him to offer a response to the world he inhabits, but it is a weak one. Hence Donald's lack of critical sense, or rather Coover's at this stage of his development as a writer, prevents "The Square-Shooter and the Saint" and "Dinner with the King of England" from offering a serious comment on the adult world at large.

Nevertheless, there is something to learn from these stories that is near the core of all the works this study has examined so far, namely, that relying on any single perspective, as Donald does almost by nature, produces only a false perspective of life. Similarly, those readers who insist on retaining the limited perspectives inherited from traditional approaches to literature will feel as out of place in Coover's world as Donald does in the Royal Palace, or perhaps, as Donald did in "The Square-Shooter and the Saint," they will love what they do not understand. That which is familiar in Coover's works are self-reflective, ironic comments on the literature that has preceded them. From these familiar fictional elements, such as plot, character, theme, and symbol, Coover creates combinations that afford his readers a broader literary perspective. Because Coover's stories ask the reader to be aware of the invented, fictional nature of the works he is reading, the effect of experiencing his fictions is much like being within the frame of a painting and observing it from a distance at the same time. In the works that are to come, Coover will improve upon the narrative constructs he has explored in these early fictions and learn to incorporate into them the genuine sense of human emotions he first expressed in "The Brother" and "J's Marriage."

CHAPTER 2

From Brunists to Baseball

I The Origin of the Brunists

"**B**EFORE *BRUNISTS*, I had never thought about writing a novel. I don't know why, but it had never quite occurred to me. I thought I would always go on writing these stories. It wasn't until I was nearly thirty that I first thought, 'Well, what about a book?' I had several ideas—one of them, the J. Henry Waugh short story on which *The Universal Baseball Association* was based, had already been written and, I believe, published by then. There were other possibilities, further out, that I am still struggling with today, and I was intending to go straight ahead with them. But partly because of pressure from friends, agents, and editors, and the friendly reception of my first published story, 'Blackdamp,' a mine disaster story, in *The Noble Savage,* I went to work instead on *The Brunists*" (Gado, p. 148).

The fact that Coover's first novel is not organized according to one fictional kind but follows a variety of modes—novel of manners, psychological novel, social satire, fabulous story, religious parody, realistic novel, black humor novel, soap opera, and radical protest novel—may be one reason why the responses of its first reviewers were so mixed. William Mathes of *Book Week* praised *The Origin of the Brunists* as

a remarkable achievement of imagination, concern, and sheer creative force—sustained and elaborated from beginning to end. . . . Mr. Coover's characterizations are sharply wrought and remarkably multi-dimensional. . . . The handling of so many characters so masterfully is virtually unknown in first novels. In addition, Mr. Coover sustains the intensity and readability of his narrative, joining and moving his people and their dilemmas toward a final effort that is compelling and lasting. . . . This is fiction as it should be, the product of high emotion and dedicated talent: real hot with life in conflict, filled with the bizarre and commonplace.[1]

On the other hand, Bruno McAndrews of *Best Sellers* wrote:

This is a vicious and dirty piece of writing. Reading a book like this (a heavy task) makes one melancholy about the future of American fiction. Nothing in the decadent literature of ancient Rome is any worse, or even as bad. But what is the purpose of this explosion in a cesspool? It is nothing less, in my opinion, than an attack on Christianity. For at the head of every chapter dealing with the insane doings of the sect, there is a quotation from Scripture, more or less related. The parallel is obvious—this were [*sic*] the beginning of Christianity. . . . It is the product of an overheated brain.[2]

In spite of the general perplexity among reviewers, who seemed to have been overwhelmed and occasionally polarized by the variety of genres and themes that Coover incorporates into his novel, *The Origin of the Brunists* did receive some accurate criticism. Emile Capouya, for example, read Coover's book as an attempt "to revive the naturalistic novel for serious literary purposes by grafting on to it fantastic, surreal, and hysterical elements."[3] This combination of realism and artifice is first recognized in the styles Coover employs to narrate his story. At times he writes as if he were a realist: "There was a comforting fullness about the room. Elaine Collins, listening to the high school basketball game while she ironed, wished to be there, yet she knew she was always frightened outside the house, and once out would wish to be back" (*OB*, p. 47).[4] No sooner does the reader become secure in this distinctive but conventional style, however, than Coover discards his realist mode for an artificial one. The high-school basketball game that Elaine is listening to on the radio the narrator describes as if it were a masque: "Exchange of roles as Blacks fade to enact static counterparts to Reds now bearing down in interstitched con-figurations. Red One crosses the meridian, confronts tableau of Blacks, slows, signals placement: Red Two to his left, Red Three to center, Red Four and Five to the corners" (*OB*, p. 49). Coover's combination of realist and artificial modes, then, indicates his intention to keep the traditional novel alive by infusing it with a variety of new techniques. Without following the example of European novelists like Robbe-Grillet, who abandoned the traditional novel for more experimental forms, or blindly accepting the declarations of Susan Sontagg, Norman Mailer, and Leslie Fiedler, who have classified the conventional novel as obsolete, Coover manages to depart from the traditional novel without adopting an antinovelist style. Hence Coover can mock the traditional novel as being no longer viable while simultaneously employing its conventions in vitally new ways. The result, *The Origin of the Brunists,* represents a significant innovation in the development of the American novel. "I thought of it, a bit, as paying dues. I didn't feel I had the right to move into more presumptuous fictions until I could prove I could handle the form as it now was in the world. In a sense, the trip down into the mine was my submerging of myself into the novel experience and then coming out again with my own revelations. In the process, I turned it into my kind of book" (Gado, p. 148).

In addition to giving the traditional novel a new direction, *The Origin of the Brunists* offers a summation of the narrative processes and issues Coover explored in his earlier works as well as a comprehensive view of his later interests: "The basic concerns that are in everything I write are also in that book—though they look a little different, they are still there" (Gado, p. 148). Long and complicated, Coover's first novel presents a host of over twenty characters, both realistic and exaggerated, and almost as many plots, which are narrated through monologues, streams of consciousness, letters to the editor, religious sermons, voices from the supernatural, and an interesting form of third-person narration that occasionally shifts into the language of the character being described.

That these voices include high-school students, coal miners, newspapermen, religious fanatics, businessmen, and more is a testament to Coover's adept ear for dialogue, which seems to fail him occasionally. It is difficult to believe, for example, that newspapermen can wax as eloquent as "The first thing you know they're whamming away in rhythm and she's clutching him in the ass and warbling his goddamn name and they both come in a tremendous explosion and collapse in a tremor of secondary spasms" (*OBB*, p. 113). Similarly, nurses are not usually prone to write: "At one point during the Last Judgment, at a peculiarly tense and difficult moment, someone present released a thundering, monumental—if not indeed mystical—fart. It was not, however, as efficacious as its historic reputation might have led one to expect" (*OB*, p. 437). Interestingly, Coover does not care if his characters' voices agree with their personalities and backgrounds any more than if his storytelling techniques coincide with traditional narrative forms. In fact, he purposely juxtaposes his characters' voices with their stereotyped personalities in order to make the reader pay closer attention to what is being said: "The first and primary and essential talent of the artist is to reach the emotions . . . great art always must reach there first. But it's a little hard to know what reaching the emotions means. It doesn't necessarily mean learning a skill and doing it as perfectly as you can. It may mean only a kind of sense of reaching people on a visceral level" (Hertzel, pp. 26–27).

The Origin of the Brunists opens with a quotation from the Revelation to John, "Write what you see in a book and send it to the Seven Churches" (*OB*, p. 11), and Coover's analogue to the founding of Christianity may be considered a satiric response to that command. Nevertheless, Coover's attitude toward his satire is neither bitter nor frustrated. Recognizing the need for illusion in a world that is often unreasonable, Coover demonstrates a genuine compassion for the tendency in people to project the chaotic events of their lives into fictions they believe are accurate explanations of reality. Coover's satire on Christianity, then, transcends the functions of exposure and ridicule to achieve a seriocomic vision of man's refusal to accept fiction and reality for what they are.

In the prologue to his novel, Coover immediately establishes an ironic contrast between fiction and reality. As he did in "Klee Dead" and "In a Train Station," Coover begins his story after most of the events he chronicles have taken place. Through the eyes of the narrator, who focuses his attention on Hiram Clegg, a recent convert to the Brunist religion, the reader receives an unclear picture of an event that is about to take place. Something important is about to happen, but not even Hiram, who is soon to be a bishop in the church, knows what. The Final Judgment is a strong possibility. Whatever is going to occur, however, the news media are there to broadcast it to the world. Prepared for something momentous, Hiram is surprised to find himself watching the seemingly anticlimactic death of a young woman who has been hit by an automobile. When the woman is identified as the sister of the Brunists' founder, the circumstances surrounding her death gradually become incorporated into a religious myth that differs markedly from the scene Hiram has witnessed.

The discrepancy that exists between what happened on the night of Marcella Bruno's death and the myth that has been created from those events is underscored by the narrator's use of qualifying terms such as "some seemed to remember" and "there were those who recalled" whenever he speaks of an occurrence that contradicts Hiram's eyewitness account. By establishing in the prologue the fact that the events described in the rest of the novel have already become legends, Coover offers his readers the opportunity to compare his narrator's more objective view of the founding of the Brunist religion with the myths that later developed.

The plot of *The Origin of the Brunists* is generated by a disaster that traps ninety-eight men in the Deepwater No. 9 Coalmine. Giovanni Bruno, the one man who is saved, becomes the center of a religious cult, the Brunists. Recording for his newspaper and history the coincidences that convince the Brunists that their prophet, whose brain has been damaged by the carbon monoxide he inhaled in the mine, is a voice from the supernatural is Jusstin "Tiger" Miller, whose newspaper's coverage of the sect brings them international attention. Although Miller is the cult's composite of the four Evangelists, his interest in the Brunists is centered on the good story they make and his affection for Bruno's daughter, Marcella. The book reaches its climax on the Mount of Redemption as the Brunists await a supernatural event. Marcella, whom Miller cannot persuade to leave the cult for him, dies after being struck down by an automobile driven by one of the Brunists. The victim of an ax-wielding fanatic, Miller also dies, but Coover later resurrects him and shifts his analogy of Christ's sacrifice from Marcella to the reporter, who is also the cult's Judas after having betrayed the sect in a special issue of his newspaper. While he lies crucified in traction, Miller's nurse and girlfriend, Happy Bottom, pierces his side with a needle and accepts her Christ-figure's invitation to start a private little cult of their own. Though every bit as humorous as this plot outline indicates, *The Origin of the Brunists* is more than a 440-page lampoon on Christianity. For Coover the book represents a successful fusing of the ideas about writing and human nature that gave philosophical weight to his earlier works with an emotional depth they frequently lacked. For the reader, Coover's novel is a definition of man and his plight to make sense out of the world he inhabits. In order to understand Coover's perception of human nature and how effectively he presents it, however, an investigation of the text that goes beneath the surface of plot and obvious satire is necessary.

The opening chapter of the Brunists' story initiates the narrator's shift from a third- to a first-person perspective, thereby creaating a sense of immediacy that the distanced, analytical voice of the prologue lacked. Deeply rooted in the realistic conventions of the nineteenth-century novel, the narrator shifts his focus from the Deepwater No. 9 Coalmine to the high-school basketball game and back again as he introduces most of the novel's characters. Coover, as he does in his portrayal of the basketball game, describes the mine explosion, which is caused by a cigarette being lighted in an exposed area, in a style not usually associated with realistic literature:

> THERE WAS LIGHT and
> post drill leaped smashed the
> turned over whole goddamm car kicking
> felt it in his ears, grabbed his bucket, and turned
>   from the face,
> but then the second
> "Hank! Hank Harlowe! I can't see nothin! Hank?" (*OB*, p. 40)

This sudden interruption of the novel's conventional style blasts the reader into a heightened awareness of what has occurred in the mine and offers him as close an approximation to a real explosion as literature can provide.

Coover's realism, however, covers more territory than stylistic innovation and workers' dialogue. After Giovanni Bruno is rescued from the mine, the narrator sets several subplots in motion that provide the background from which the founding of the cult can be understood. Critics have accused Coover of creating a potboiler in these subplots, which include most of the sensational elements usually associated with small towns, but a close analysis reveals the necessity of establishing a foundation that makes the rise of the Brunist cult credible. This is not the story of religious fanatics in what Webster Schott describes as a "small town berserk with holiness,"[5] but rather the attempts of ordinary people to answer the oldest question in man's experience, "Why?" Perhaps the saving of just one man is not just chance. Perhaps it is a sign of some kind that, when correctly interpreted, might lead to an understanding of why catastrophes such as this one occur. Are they part of an overall plan? Probably not, but coincidences, reactions to these questions, and Justin Miller's newspaper encourage a small group of West Condon's citizens to try to find some justification for the death of so many men. It is this temptation to justify what has no purpose that leads to the founding of the Brunists, a cult of people whose sense of reality has been threatened by a catastrophe and who in desperation create a fiction to explain what has happened in terms that confirm their already-held viewpoints of life's meaning. When Justin Miller brings Clara Collins a note that her husband was writing to her just before he died, the hysterical woman exclaims, "If'n he died like that, they must be a reason! The Good Lord would not take Ely away if'n they weren't no reason! Would He? . . . Why did Ely die and his partner live? *What is God tryin' to tell me* . . ." (*OB*, p. 88). Clara looks for an answer in Ely's message, which says that "We will stand Together before our Lord the 8th of" (*OB*, p. 96). Because she cannot decode the message by herself, Clara brings it to Abner Baxter, the minister who has replaced her husband at the Church of the Nazarene. Baxter, made nervous by the distraught woman's hysterical appeals for him to provide her with an interpretation of the message and momentarily distracted by his mischievous children, mutters something about "the end of all things is at hand" (*OB*, p. 96), which Clara recognizes as the answer to her question. Ely, she intuitively surmises, was telling her when the end of the world will be, but he never completed the date. Abner explains that the explosion occurred on the eighth of the month and that Ely was probably dating the letter, but Clara has already internalized the original interpretation of the message and, in her mind, the true import of its contents. That Ely never put a period at the end of his note, she says, is proof that he was interested in more important matters than the date of his own demise. Having placed her husband's death within a context she can understand, Clara's view of reality is no longer threatened. She feels comforted. When Bruno is eventually released from the hospital in which he was recuperating from gas inhalation, a group of people interested in the same sort of security that Clara has found seek him out.

This cause-and-effect mentality, which the narrator of "Klee Dead" has called a disease of the Western mind, is at the core of the myths contemporary man has inherited. Religious myths, for example, provide people like Clara Collins with a scheme from which all events can be understood. A different kind of myth but one which operates just as effectively in Coover's novel is numerology. Rooted in the same preoccupation with causality as the religious myths, this more scientific handle on life explores the numerological connections between numbers and events. Ralph Himebaugh, West Condon's file-cabinet lawyer, believes that all the events that occur in the universe can be explained according to mathematical formulas. Through the compilation of these formulas, patterns emerge that provide a numerological basis from which the past can be understood and the future predicted. Unlike Clara, Himebaugh seeks to understand the meaning of events from the empirical data at hand rather than from inherited myths about the supernatural. Unfortunately, Ralph's formulas are as far removed from reality as Clara's myths:

The number ninety-seven, the number of the dead, was itself unbelievably relevant. Not only did it take its place almost perfectly in the concatenation of disaster figures he had been recording, but it contained internal mysteries as well: nine, after all was the number of the mine itself, and seven, pregnant integer out of all divination, was the number of trapped miners. The number between nine and seven, eight, was the date of the explosion, and the day of the rescue was eleven, two one's or two, the difference between nine and seven. Nine and seven added to sixteen, whose parts, one and six, again added to . . . seven. (*OB*, p. 188)

As a result of the data he amasses over a period of four years, Himebaugh finds himself lacking only a final calculation of the value *x* on his disaster parabola. What Ralph's graphs cannot do for him, however, Brunist mystic Eleanor Norton does: "She hesitated as though afraid to continue. A small sob caught in her chest. *'The end of the world.'* 'Oh no!' cried Himebaugh. 'I thought so!'" (*OB*, p. 211).

Whereas Clara Collins receives her interpretations of the world's chaos from myths and Ralph Himbaugh learns to understand the world through numerological systems, Mrs. Eleanor Norton, a local schoolteacher with an unflattering employment record, is a religious person whose ideas about human nature come to her directly from a voice in the supernatural. Eleanor has difficulty, however, relating her messages, which of course are nothing more than unconscious responses to her own psychic needs, to the particulars of everyday life. Spreading the word of Domiron to her students, for example, usually results in her losing her job and being asked to move with her husband from the neighborhood in which they are living at the time. Through Ralph, Eleanor finds a person whose empirically based constructions support her vision of reality. She, in turn, provides Ralph with an end toward which he can direct his computations. Through the spiritual relationship that blossoms between Eleanor and Ralph, Coover provides his readers with a humorous parody of the deductive and inductive reasoning processes as the two Brunists work hard at projecting their distorted psyches on Clara Collins and similarly disturbed members of the community.

The source through which Eleanor, with support from Ralph and Clara, manipulates the Brunists is, of course, Giovanni Bruno, whose name may be an ironic variation of Giordano Bruno, a sixteenth-century relativist. His brain damaged by carbon monoxide, Bruno is little more than a vegetable when Eleanor visits him in the hospital. Through her peculiar use of the deductive reasoning process, Eleanor suspects that the real Bruno died in the mine and that the body that was rescued is being inhabited by a being from another world.

While Coover's portrayal of Eleanor and Ralph borders on farce, his development of the people who react to the Brunists is somewhat more complicated. Ted Cavanaugh, a local banker who is afraid of the mine shutting down and the financial losses that will result, tries to attract some outside interest in West Condon by publicizing Bruno's release from the hospital. Although Cavanaugh dislikes the Brunists and recognizes them as the disturbed people that they are, he is very much like them in his willingness to create fictions about Bruno to satisfy his own ends. By making Bruno a hero of the community and a symbol of its perseverance, however, Cavanaugh unwittingly helps the cause of the Brunists, whom he is trying to run out of town through his Common Sense Committee.

Equally displeased with the Brunists is Reverend Baxter, who sees the cult as a threat to the spiritual welfare of his congregation and consequently a potential danger to his own financial and popular security. Baxter denounces the cult but, like Cavanaugh, inadvertently helps them. As was true with the early Christians, who faced persecution at the hands of the Romans, Baxter's attacks only make them stronger in their newfound faith. Furthermore, Baxter's criticism of the new religious sect unconsciously inspires his mischievous children to play pranks on the Brunists. A charred hand, which the children have taken from the remains of one of the mine's victims, soon becomes a symbol associated with their practical jokes, some of which, the burning of a Brunist house, for example, are not so funny. Instead of recognizing the human maliciousness that lies behind the pranks, however, the Brunists interpret what occurs as messages that they translate and incorporate into the myth they are creating. Forced to seek each other's company for protection as well as spiritual support, the Brunists form a communal core that Coover believes is at the center of religious life: ". . . We get our idea of religion, of a something larger than ourselves, by way of communal meetings. We live isolated lives, but when we come together in a group, . . . we get a sense of being part of something beyond our individual existences. In part, this is repressive—in that individual freedom diminishes markedly; in part, there is an exhilaration in feeling the new power of the group" (Gado, p. 156).

Like Ted Cavanaugh, Tiger Miller recognizes the group neurosis of the Brunists and uses the cult to further his own interests: he needs some good stories for his marginally successful newspaper. Because of the *Chronicle's* banner headline: "MIRACLE IN WEST CONDON," which Miller wrote "just to wow the homefolks" (*OB*, p. 85), the Brunists allow him to attend their communal meetings. When the newspaperman initiates a genuine love relationship with Marcella Bruno, the prophet-miner's daughter, the Brunists make him their scribe. Miller keeps the minutes of the meetings and publishes articles in the *Chronicle* that are sympathetic if not favorable to the Brunist cause. The information that is the most damaging to the cult, the reporter saves for a special pictorial issue that he has in mind. Miller resists publishing the exposé, however, until he can convince Marcella that the Brunists are a collection of disturbed

people and that she should leave them for him. Unfortunately.
Marcella believes in the Brunists and is offended by Miller's
proposal. Realizing that he has overestimated Marcella's willingness to respond to him or reason, Miller decides to teach all the
Brunists a lesson and publish his special report on the cult one
week before the day on which they have predicted the Final
Judgment or the Coming of the White Bird will occur. As
Cavanaugh and Baxter did before him, however, Miller, through
his exposé, contributes to the cause he is attacking. Because he
has sold his story to newspapers and magazines all over the
country, Miller has spread the Brunist word. From all the corners
of the country and, indeed, the world, people, who need the
crutch of fiction and the illusion of order to help them
understand the experiences of life that are frequently beyond
limited comprehension, respond to Miller's story. On the
expected Day of Judgment, the Brunists, their numbers swelled
by the publicity they have received, march to a Mount of
Redemption that is populated by media people and curiosity-
seekers. Appropriately, Elaine Collins, the teenage daughter of
Clara Collins, tells her boyfriend that she wishes she could go
home and watch the important event on television, as if
whatever occcurs is more real there. Of course the end of the
world comes only for Marcella Bruno, who is hit by an
automobile, but Miller comes perilously close to losing his life
also as the angry Brunists attack their Judas and ironically turn
the "Tiger" into a sacrificial lamb. As he had done with Marcella,
Miller overestimated the affect his reasonable disclosures about
the cult would have on its members. Myths like the one the
Brunists create, Coover is saying, are so emotionally centered as
to be beyond reason. When they are combated, they must be met
on their own grounds: "The force of myth and mythopeic
thought is with us for all time. The crucial beliefs of people are
mythic in nature; whether at the level of the Cinderella story or
of the Resurrection, the language is mythopeic rather than
rational. To try to apply reason to such beliefs is like trying to
solve a physics problem by psychoanalysis" (Gado, p. 152).

Because of the publicity they have received, the Brunists are
able to establish themselves as a major religion with a liturgy,
martyrs, a persecution history, symbolic costumes, secret hand-
shakes, prophecies, bishops such as Hiram Clegg, rituals, and
monetary donations from all over the world. In a few years, as

the reader already knows from Coover's prologue, the story of Giovanni Bruno and his first disciples will become a sacred tradition. That this tradition bears a strong resemblance to Christianity is not, of course, coincidental.

In contrast with the Brunists and the self-interested townspeople who unwittingly contribute to the cult's cause is Happy Bottom, an earthy pagan who loves her body and Miller's and whose message is that the important things in life are in the here and now. More of a voice for Coover than a nurse in love with a newspaper reporter from a small town, Happy Bottom views the Brunists and the community's reaction to them with indifference, but when spurned by Miller for Marcella Bruno, the clever woman sends messages about the afterlife to her lover that bear the mark of "The Black Hand":

The next supplicant, a virgin who shall here be otherwise nameless, was brought before the Judge. Her virginity, of course, was not a possession (the Judgement itself made property an absurd contradiction), but rather of the essence, a thing happily forever renewable, if in fact with use it ever aged.
   —And why do you wish to be admitted to heaven?
   —What is Heaven?
   —Why Heaven is where I am.
   —And where are you?
   —I have said.
   —And so have I.
The Judge smiled and because, to tell the truth, there had never been a Heaven before, the Judge and the virgin forthwith created one and had a Hell of a good time doing it. . . . (*OB*, p. 350)

For Happy Bottom, and for Coover, apparently, God, if there is one, is not in the image man has created him to be. At best, he is human and has nothing to do with the guilt, fear, and punishment associated with the Brunists and other religions.

Though the central focus of *The Origin of the Brunists* is on religious myths, Coover's first novel is also a commentary on history, which, like religion, fictionalizes and reveres human experience. Except perhaps for its imposition of a specific time, the events of history, says Coover, are not much different from myths. Both stem from man's desire to place his experiences within a context he can understand. Consequently, "the real power of historical events," says William Gass, lies in their descriptions; only by virtue of their passage into language can they continue to occur, and once recorded (even if no more than gossip), they become peculiarly atemporal, residing in that shelved up present which passes for time in a library. . . . What we remember of our own past depends very largely on what of it we've put our tongue to telling and retelling. It's our words, roughly, we remember; oblivion claims the rest—forgetfulness. Historians make more history than the men they write about, and because we render our experience in universals, experience becomes repetitious (for if events do not repeat, accounts do), and time doubles back in confusion like a hound which has lost its scent.[6]

Tainted by the desperate needs that created it, history, like myth, has no more meaning than men assign to it. Having given a reporter from United Press International a story he made up about the explosion in the mine, Miller states that his tale is the kind of document of which history is made. Rushing to publish the story he believes is fact, the reporter represents those weaknesses in man that work against a true perception of reality. As fiction making its way in the world as fact, history and religion amount to little more than conveniences designed by people to maintain the status quo of self-blindness and prevent them from discovering the significant truths of their existence. " 'History,' " says West Condon miner Vince Bonali, " 'is like a big goddam sea, Sal, and here we are, bobbing around on it, a buncha poor bastards who can't swim, seasick, lost, unable to see past the next goddam wave, not knowing where the hell it's taking us if it takes us anywhere at all' " (*OB*, p. 330).

One way of imposing an order on reality that is not damaging in the ways that religion and history are is through games, a seemingly secondary but equally important issue in *The Origin of the Brunists* and many of Coover's other works. Closely related to Coover's interest in games is his theory of creating fictions, namely, that they are an enjoyable, useful, even necessary way of enriching the life experience, but they should never be regarded as truth or dogma. Games, for example, provide Tiger Miller with a sense of order and a perspective on life that Vince Bonali lacks:

Games are what kept Miller going. Games, and the pacifying of mind and organs. Miller perceived existence as a loose concatenation of separate and ultimately inconsequential instants, each colored by the actions that preceded it, but each possessed of a small wanton freedom of its own. Life, then, was a series of adjustments to these actions and, if one kept his sense of humor and produced as many of these actions as possible, adjustment was easier. (*OB*, pp. 141-42)

Miller's view, by his own definition, contradicts the historical perspective that relationships between events can be explained and an order imposed on them. By believing in games, Miller can create a system of order that provides meaning in his life but only within the context of what he knows is a fiction. His desire to create and participate in games stems from the same needs that drive people to establish religions and record history. The difference, however, lies in the fact that Miller's games make no claims to truth or objectivity.

Recognizing the fictive elements that reside in the roots of all religions, Miller's initial interest in the Brunists is inspired by his willingness to participate in what he sees as a game. Later, when Reverend Edwards accuses Miller of printing material that might be "adversely affecting the impressionable young," he asks the reporter if it ever occurs to him that

"these are human lives—one-time human lives—you're toying with!"
"Sure, what else?"
"But to make a game out of—"
Miller laughed. "You know Edwards, it's the one thing you and I have got in common." (*OB*, p. 264)

The point Coover makes here is obvious: Edwards's religion is as much of a fictitious manipulation of human beings as the game Miller is playing with the Brunists and the people of West Condon. Nevertheless, Edwards has been playing the game of religion longer than Miller, whose experiences on the Mount of Redemption later underscore Edwards' comment that the "'only difference . . . is that I know what I'm doing'" (*OB*, p. 264). That Miller has incorrectly calculated the effect of his game-playing is further evidenced by the fact that his reports on the Brunists, rather than bringing their activities to a halt, increase their numbers and ensure their continuance beyond the dates of their unfulfilled prophecies.

Behind the game-player, Miller, of course, stands the game-maker, Coover, whose innovative narrative techniques reveal a predilection for entertainment that is similar to the reporter's.

The name of Coover's game in *The Origin of the Brunists,* as it
was in "Seven Exemplary Fictions" and "The Sentient Lens," is
"Expectations Denied." As has been mentioned earlier in this
chapter, Coover begins his first book in a prose style that is
characteristic of nineteenth-century realist novels. At times
Coover, as he did in "J's Marriage," employs a narrator that
sounds almost Jamesian: "Hiram was not ignorant of, nor did he
shy from, the recognition of the sensual excitation that accompanied the spiritual one. . . . And yet, though perhaps it
enhanced the fervor of their songs and prayers, there was a total
chastity, not merely of action but of thought, pervading them all"
(*OB,* p. 22). Throughout the novel, however, Coover crashes
through the surface of his realist mode to describe such things as
the mine explosion in a Joycean stream-of-consciousness style,
and a basketball game in the form of a masque that includes stage
directions. Marcella, who has a somewhat abnormal attachment
to the Brunist myth, is described throughout the novel in a
correspondingly artificial prose that is heightened by the fact
that it is written in italics:

*She sees her shadow as the light sweeps down on her from behind. She
tries to enclose herself in its sweep. She spreads wide her arms to hold it
back. Suddenly . . . It comes! she cries. God is here! she laughs. And
she spins whirls embraces light leaps heaving her bathing in light her
washes and as she flows laughs His Presence light! stars burst sky burns
with absolute light! and.* (*OB,* p. 389)

Also punctuating Coover's realist style are radio broadcasts,
religious sermons, messages from Domiron, who resides in the
supernatural and speaks through Eleanor Norton and Giovanni
Bruno, and lyrics that run the gamut from tradition hymns such
as "Amazing Grace" to folk songs created by the Brunists:

> White Dove will mourn in sorrow,
> And the willows bow down their heads,
> I live my life in sorrow,
> Since Mother and Daddy are dea-ea-ead! (*OB,* p. 357)

Occasionally Coover will begin an episode in a serious tone of
voice in order to create a level of suspense that he will later
burlesque:

He reaches up, grasps something. "That's odd," he says softly. The others crowd around. He is holding what seems to be a sort of tag, tied by a string to a bulky object above. He adjusts his glasses on his nose, squints, reads: PULL ME . . . "What should we do," he whispers in his tiny voice. Ben Wosznick strides forward, takes a look at the tag, gives it a yank. There is a soft pop and then hundreds of white feathers cascade gently around their heads. "The White Bird!" cry several women at once. (*OB*, p. 333)

Coover's best narrative trick, however, is reserved for his having Tiger Miller pass on to his reward at the hand of the Brunists on the Mount of Redemption and then resurrecting him in a subsequent chapter.

In the same way as he develops a style that fails to match consistently his readers' expectations, Coover also creates characters whom he introduces realistically but later gives a voice that does not correspond with their personalities. Italian miner Vince Bonali's vision of history, newspaper reporter Lou Jones's too carefully worded stories, and nurse Happy Bottom's wry comments on the after life are not true to the characters Coover has created; nevertheless, what they say is given all that more attention as the reader learns to regard them as mouthpieces for Coover. The decidedly most interesting and multi-dimensional of Coover's characters is, of course, Justin Miller, whose first name may contain an ironic allusion to the second-century Christian apologist, St. Justin. Miller's running of the newspaper office is comical, his love for Marcella Bruno is pathetic, his exploitation of the Brunists is deplorable, and his affair with Happy Bottom is deceitful but human. An interesting mixture of Judas and Jesus, a tiger and a lamb, Miller contributes as much to the enjoyment of Coover's readers as he does to the Brunist cause.

Staring at X rays of his fractured clavicle, right thumb and left humerus, which Happy held out for him to see one morning while one of her buddies gave him an enema, . . . and deep despair sprayed up his ass and inundated his body. "Why did you bother, Happy?" he asked. He expected her to make some crack, but instead she only smiled and said, "I don't know. I guess because I like the way you laugh." Yes, there was that, Not the void within and ahead, but the immediate living space between the two. The plug was out of him with a soft gurgle. "My message to the world," he said. (*OB*, p. 435)

Miller's message, and Coover's, is that what's important in life lies not in the cosmic, supernatural, and eternal but in the immediate, everyday, and human.

While writing *The Origin of the Brunists,* Coover developed several characters who emphasized the disparity that exists between the cosmic and the everyday, but because they encompassed more than he was prepared to have his readers assimilate, they were excluded from the novel's final draft.

Five years after the publication of *The Origin of the Brunists,* however, Coover resurrected a jetisoned character from his desk drawer and published *The Water Pourer,* which begins:

Life for Patterson, in a word, is dull and useless; it isn't h, it's something less than, and that is the number one fivestar superhistorical axiom. Nights he can't sleep, days he can't wake up. It's all he can do mornings to heave his fortyfive-year-old rump out of the old chenille and drag it off to the highschool to teach history—off to the horse stool to breach hysteris, as he once phrased it for the guys on the church lawn, getting a very lacklustre response for it considering the time it had taken him to think it up. Fortyfive? out goes the old goat one bitter day and in comes the grim waterpourer: thirty godblessed days and he'll drop from sight into "the late forties." On the way out, Charlie. Don't think about it. Do things. (*WP,* p. 3)[7]

One of the things that Patterson does to avoid watching the clock of his life is accept a dinner invitation from Annie Pompa to celebrate his birthday. Annie, an overweight Italian looking for a husband, works with Patterson on the *Chronicle.* She has a genuine affection for the teacher that he uses to buttress up his frequently staggering ego. Patterson prepares for what he thinks will be a quiet celebration with Annie by downing a few predinner drinks at a local gin mill. By the time he reaches Annie's house, however, he is suffering the effects of more than a few drinks. To his surprise, Annie has invited seven women and her brother-in-law to participate in the festive dinner that she has made. Through the meal's courses, Annie's guests become familiar with Patterson. Although they noticed when he arrived that he had been drinking, they are drinking now also and less inclined to think ill of him. They forgive him for making them wait an hour for their dinner, try to ignore the fact that he is a Presbyterian, and make jokes about his being Annie's beau. The food, meanwhile, returns to Patterson some of his senses, but, at the same time, gradually removes from him the control of his bladder. Afraid to walk doubled-over to the bathroom, Patterson urinates at the table and, shortly afterwards, makes a quick exit for his room at Mrs. Battles's. On his way home to the room in which he has been living the life of a man's man for twenty years, Patterson's thoughts are far from the cosmic "Ply 'em, plumb 'em, and plug 'em" (*WP*, p. 12) visions on which he had focused earlier in the evening. "Tick. Tick. Tick. Nice, Charlie, nice. Superhistorical. . . . Wet pants stiff from the cold and they rasp against his skin. And on home. Home forever to Mrs. B. And boiled eggs. Oh man. Into the late forties. Plip ploop plop" (*WP*, p. 22).

Through the characters he develops, the story he tells, and the narrative artifices he constructs in *The Origin of the Brunists* and *The Water Pourer*, Coover emphasizes the inventive nature of his books, shows how fiction can be turned into fact, exposes man's fear to discover himself, and delineates the willingness of people to accept as truths the myths of religion and history. Ironically, he often sounds as dogmatic as the institutional voices he is debunking. Nevertheless he is forgiven, for, in Tiger Miller's words, he tells a good story, one that merited the 1966 William Faulkner Award.

II   The Universal Baseball Association, Inc., J. Henry Waugh, Prop.

When *The Universal Baseball Association, Inc., J. Henry Waugh, Prop.* was first published, Coover received an amazing number of letters from people who were surprised to discover that someone beside themselves was interested in baseball games that were played with cards and dice. "I had thought it was a private idea, a private book, but I soon learned that sort of activity was rather general. One guy who had read the review— but not the book—sent a letter in which he remembered his leagues, the players' names, their batting averages, everything— and, considering he'd done this before World War I, in incredible detail.

"Now they even have computers doing it. They compile tapes with all the parameters—down to factors like temperament and stamina—and they distribute the printouts. It's grown to be quite a network. There is even going to be a convention of baseball parlor game players in Philadelphia. Somehow, these enthusiasts have fostered the hope that I should be the secretary for some such organization. It's been a bit of a harassment" (Gado, p. 150).

The Universal Baseball Association, Inc., J. Henry Waugh, Prop., like *The Origin of the Brunists*, is primarily concerned with man's need to create fictions that give his world a sense of order and meaning. These fictions may be highly artificial, as in the case of games or mathematical formulas, or they may be more subjective, such as when they appear in the forms of myth, religion, and history. When man forgets his role as a creator of fiction, however, and begins to accept the works of his imagination as fact, he finds himself imprisoned and manipulated by the very perspectives that he constructed. Half the length of his first novel but much more interesting, *The Universal Baseball Association, Inc.* evolved from "The Second Son," a short story that appeared several years before *The Origin of the Brunists*. "After the story (which is, essentially, the second chapter of the book) was written, I felt that I hadn't gotten everything out of the metaphor, that I hadn't yet fully understood it. So over the years that followed I set about playing with the images, working out the Association history, searching out the structure that seemed to be hidden in it" (Gado, p. 148). The result is a fascinating story about the loss of self an artist can experience through the projections of his own imagination.

"The Second Son" is narrated on two levels, each of which is psychologically unconvincing and reduces the story to a slightly more serious version of "The Secret Life of Walter Mitty." Like the narrator of "The Square-Shooter and the Saint" and "Dinner with the King of England," the speaker of "The Second Son" describes his characters from a detached point of view that prevents him from successfully intermingling their lives with those his protagonist creates. Henry Waugh, an accountant who is bored with his job and the people he knows, creates a baseball game that he plays with dice on an imaginary field. The game and its players, each of whom has a mythified biography, are so exciting that they soon overshadow the reality of Henry's drab existence. In time, Henry's preoccupation with the form of escape he has invented effects his performance at work. Gradually losing sight of the artificial nature of his game, Henry begins to believe in the existence of his players, one of whom, Damon Rutherford, becomes something like a second son to him.

Having projected into the young pitcher an image of what he would like to be, Henry suffers a breakdown when a roll of the dice determines that Rutherford has been killed by a pitched ball.

Coover's second novel maintains the same premise that is outlined here, but he replaces his limited third-person narrator with one that effectively melds the reader's perception of Henry's real and imaginary worlds. Whereas the narrator of the story keeps fact distinct from fiction, that of the novel blends the two by allowing his readers to enter the mind of Henry and see his characters as he sees them:

Mounting the stairs, Henry heard the roar of the crowd, saw them take their seats. Bowlegged old Maggie Everts trundled out of the Haymaker dugout to replace Hill. That gave cause for a few more warm-up pitches, so Henry slowed, took the steps one at a time. Law grinned, nodded at old Maggie, stuffed a chaw of gum into his cheek. . . . "Awright! now come on you guys! a little action!" Henry shouted, Bancroft shouted, clapping his hands, and the Pioneers kept the pepper up, they hollered in the stands. (*UBA*, pp. 6–7)[8]

At times the narrator does such a good job of intermingling Henry's illusions with his reality that he seems to confuse the proprietor of the league with the characters he has invented. When Henry goes to Pete's bar for a drink, he calls Pete "Jake" because the bartender looks like Jake Bradley, one of the association's ballplayers. As the novel progresses, the reader also enters the minds of Henry's characters and sees them as they see each other and their creator:

"I'm afraid, Gringo, I must agree with our distinguished folklorist and foremost witness to the ontological revelations of the patterns of history," intercedes (with a respectful nod to Schultz) Professor Costen Migod McCamish, Doctor of Nostology and Research Specialist in the Etiology of Homo Ludens, "and have come to the conclusion that God exists and he is a nut." (*UBA*, p. 233)

A second major difference between the story and the novel lies in the names Coover has chosen for his characters. In the story, for example, Henry's boss is called Sidney Kutz, a name with no definite associations, but in the novel the same persona becomes, more appropriately, Zifferblatt, which, in German,

means "clock face." Similarly, there is a difference between the
way Coover's protagonist chooses names for his ball players in
the story and the manner in which he selects them in the novel.
In the story, Henry spends long hours going through the New
York telephone directories. The Henry of Coover's novel, on the
other hand, chooses his names by a method of association that is
similar to the one employed by Unwilling Participant in "Panel
Game": "Everywhere he looked he saw names. His head was full
of them. Bus stop. Whistlestop. Whistlestop Busby, second base"
(*UBA*, p. 46). Though the method of choosing names varies from
the story to the novel, the significance of what his players are
called remains constant to their creator. Names do not effect the
substance of reality, but they do alter its meaning. According to
Coover, names give qualities to people, places, and things that
they do not possess. Nevertheless, once these qualities become
apparent through the names that have been given them, they are
indistinguishable from properties. Hence, whatever substance
Coover's characters possess is mythified by the name to which
they are attached.

Read in terms of the names Coover has assigned them, the
baseball players become mythified into figures of Christian
legend, and the novel, in part, is reduced to a parody similar to
the one presented in *The Origin of the Brunists*. Jock Casey,
whose initials suggest an obvious parallel to Jesus Christ, may be
seen as a sacrificial figure in spite of the fact that he bears no
more resemblance to the founder of Christianity than Tiger
Miller. J. Henry Waugh, or Jahweh, kills J.C. for having fatally
struck his "son," Damon Rutherford, in the head with a baseball
and, consequently, spoiled the redemption of their creator's
waning interest in the game. Though Damon may be seen as
something of a daemon through his defeat of Swanee Law, the
circumstances of his death inspire a group of people to establish
an order of Damonites, who think of themselves as a part of the
establishment. A good Damonite is known as a company man.
Predictably, after Jock Casey's death, a group known as the
Caseyites forms in opposition to the Damonites. The Caseyites,
as might be expected, mythify Jock's few if any individual
characteristics. These two factions in the association, which, as
its title indicates, is the universe, rise in power to replace the
Guildsmen and the Individualists. No doubt, Coover is saying,
when old ideas are no longer appealing, the mere attachment of

new names can prolong their life long after their founders have been forgotten. The irony of imaginary baseball players being awarded properties on the basis of the religious and mythic associations their names inspire is underscored by the fact that the reader's sympathies are never with the Christ-figure, but rather with the daemon.

As Professor McCamish says, Waugh is a "nut," but he knows how to create myths. By bestowing associative names, keeping statistics, creating rituals, and establishing a liturgy, he records for history the life he has breathed into his fantasy. Though the mechanics of the game may be controlled by the dice, the description of the association's history, which includes player dialogues, obituaries, scandals, the soliciting of prostitutes, nights on the town, and more, is manipulated by Henry, whose literary voices run the gamut from the inflated prose styles of the folksinger and sportswriter to the scientific objectivity of the theoretician.

As it happens with all doctrines and myths that have existed for long periods of time, however, the foundation of Henry's association begins to crumble as the novel approaches its end. The players begin taking on characteristics that Henry has not assigned to them. There are people who question the significance of the annual passion play that commemorates Damon Rutherford's and Jock Casey's deaths. Others wonder whether Rutherford and Casey ever existed, whether they are not some kind of myth. Paul Trench, a rookie catcher, wonders whether life is worth living. Fortunately for Trench, the rookie playing the part of Damon in the play gives his catcher some good advice about life and not being entrenched in the fruitless search for meaning. What counts in life, says the pitcher, are not Damonites, Caseyites, or even Brunists but the love of the game. As he does in "The Brother," "J's Marriage," "The Reunion," and *The Origin of the Brunists,* then, Coover refocuses his reader's perspective on traditional Christian myths by exposing the false patterns and meanings they inspire and substituting for them a consciousness that has been expanded by human truth.

The Universal Baseball Association, Inc. contains similarities to myths and fictions other than religion. One of these is history. Not willing to accept blindly the truth of the Damonsday passion play, Paul Trench is ambivalent toward his commitment to the baseball association. He recognizes the need for the order that history establishes, but he is dissatisfied with the various explanations offered by historians as to where meaning in life lies. Cuss McCamish, one of Paul's fellow rookies in the league, claims that history is capricious and cannot be believed. He points out that history has recorded all of the details surrounding Damon's death but has neglected to mention any of those associated with Casey's. The reader knows this to be true. Because Henry, drunk and upset, fell asleep after he killed Jock Casey, he never recorded the player's history into "the Book." A small group of players accurately conclude that history is no more than the product of an imagination. Of course, these would-be philosophers are correct, but they also offer Coover's readers a comment on the fictional process. The relationship between the players and Henry parallels that between Henry and Coover. Henry is the association's historian as Coover is Henry's. Who, then, is Coover's? If the novelist within the novel can be fictitious, cannot the novelist of the novel be also? Whether Coover, his readers, or their creator is a fiction is probably not important; what is important, however, is that man is led to the idea of a design in his world. As Coover says through Immanuel Kant in the novel's epigraph: "It is here not at all requisite to prove that such an *intellectus archetypus* is possible, but only that we are led to the idea of it" (*UBA*, p. 1).

Perhaps the most extreme extent to which a mythical association may be attached to Coover's mocking analogue of history is presented by Jackson I. Cope: "One allegory cries out for attention. UBA, USA. Rutherford for Ruth, certainly, but also for rue. The Rutherfords, leaders of the Pioneers (read 'New Frontier') are special: 'maybe it was just the name that had ennobled them, for in a way . . . they were . . . the association's first real aristocrats' " (*UBA*, p. 12). The Kennedy myth of national renewal aborted is reflected in a series of killings following upon Henry's assassination of Jock after the death of Damon. Barney Bancroft—latter-day echo of Barnaby North— eventually becomes Chancellor and is assassinated, bringing on a revolt of the Universalists (*UBA*, p. 220). The Chancellor in Year LVI is, like Henry, a Legalist, and, like LBJ, a paradox: "He looked old-fashioned, but he had an abiding passion for innovation. He was the most restless activist ever to take office. . . . He was coldly calculating, yet supremely loyal to old comrades" (*UBA*, p. 147). And when the season continues in an unprecedentedly gloomy and unpopular cause, like Henry he must say: " 'And there's not a goddamn thing I can do about it' " (*UBA*, p. 150). His heir and alter ego is that grand southerner, Swanee Law. Again, allegory by metonymy. We are directed to read through the layer of the accountant Jehovah the history of the United States in the 1960s, to see the sacrifice, the consequent hopeless commitment of Henry and the Chancellor as Vietnam, to hear the surge of revolution rolling in from the future.[9]

J. Henry Waugh, Prop., as his title suggests, is the prop supporting the coincidences and remarkable patterns that are imagined from them in the Universal Baseball Association. Henry has created the association to relieve the boredom of his job and assuage his feelings of loneliness and insignificance. Although he knows two people whom he can consider friends, a fellow worker and a local prostitute, he either tolerates their presence or uses them as a means through which he can play out his fantasies. In order to have an outlet for his social inadequacies, Henry creates a game that enables him to be the kind of person he would like to be in his real life. By absorbing in himself the personalities of his characters, Henry enriches his dull existence and acquires a social confidence he otherwise lacks.

In spite of Henry's success at involving himself in a fiction that protects him from the real world, Coover is not sympathetic to the idea of people withdrawing into a self-produced reality. Such a principle "would mean that literally and figuratively, a person should not read but only write, that we should have a universe of Henrys rolling their dice alone and making up worlds to live in. I've always been contentious with my writing; I've never turned away from unpleasantness in order to provide escapism" (Gado, p. 149). Henry's game, then, is more than a means by which he can escape from the tedium of his everyday life and boost his confidence. It is also an outlet for his ideas on religion, history, myth, politics, games, numerology, philosophy, and manners. Each of the players whose personality Henry develops expresses a philosophical viewpoint of his creator as well as being a fantasized projection of his psychic needs. Most of these more rounded personalities hold or have held positions of power and significance. Pitchers, managers, or chancellors, they bring out the repressed pitcher, manager, or chancellor in Henry. When Henry brings home a local prostitute, he projects his desires for her through the personality of his most attractive player, Damon Rutherford, who enables his creator to drop his guard, step out from behind his catcher's mask, and get into the game of life that reality denies him. Perhaps the least admirable of Henry's characters is Fenn McCaffree, the chancellor of the association and a partial projection of what Henry dislikes in himself and his exploitive employer, Zifferblatt. None of the three is above using anyone else to further his own ends. Henry has no interest in his fellow worker Lou Engel unless he intends to use him to alter the direction of an unappealing fantasy. Henry also manipulates the prostitute, Hettie, into playing out his fantasies, but when she looks to him to satisfy her needs, he turns his back on her.

Fenn McCaffree's assassination, then, may be interpreted as Henry's desire to eliminate Zifferblatt, but, in light of the fact that Henry is as insensitive in his own way as the two bosses, the chancellor's death may be considered as an attempt by Henry to purge himself of the Zifferblatt and McCaffree that is a part of his personality. Other characters in the association reflect various aspects of Henry's personality: Melbourne Trench is afraid of death, Rag Rooney drinks too much, Jock Casey is patient, Barney Bancroft endures, and Sycamore Flynn trembles. Most like Flynn but wanting to be like Rutherford, Henry embodies in either reality or fantasy each of his characters' personalities; unfortunately, he is not able to maintain the distinction between his projections and his real self for very long. Through the significant and powerful proprietor of these and 160 other personages, Henry soon becomes entrapped in the fantasy he has created. Speaking through the persona of Sycamore Flynn, who is lost in his own ballpark, Henry "realized, past Casey, past home plate, there was an exit. Maybe it was a way out, maybe it wasn't. But he'd never make it. It was all he wanted, but he'd never make it. He couldn't even turn around. And besides, he wasn't sure what he'd find at home plate on the way. 'I quit,' he said. But then the lights came on" (*UBA*, p. 123).

The path by which Henry goes from the creator to a slave of his own invention is short but varied. Like Tiger Miller in *The Origin of the Brunists*, Henry's attraction to games results from a lack of stimulation in his own life. One of the first games he developed was an extension of the popular board game Monopoly. Henry's version, however, employed as many as twenty-four boards and could accommodate an unlimited number of players. This proving not to be practical, Henry experimented with other paper games such as basketball, different card games, war and finance games, horse-racing, and football. Unlike Tiger Miller's games and the one played in Coover's early short story "Panel Game," however, Henry's do not include unknowing or unwilling participants. Hettie and Lou know that they are playing a game with Henry, but they are unaware of the extent to which Henry participates in it. Because Henry's games are almost purely fictional, they do not invite the kind of human reprisal that Tiger Miller's did. The favorite of Henry's games, baseball, reflects its creator's interest in numbers:

Nothing like it really. Not the actual game so much—to tell the truth, real baseball bored him—but rather the records, the statistics, the peculiar balances between the individuals and team offense and defense, strategy and luck, accident and pattern, power and intelligence. And no other activity in the world has so precise and comprehensive a history, so specific an ethic, and at the same time, strange as it seemed, so much ultimate mystery. (*UBA*, p. 45)

In other words, there is no other game that is more like life should be: a world rich in fiction that has been developed from reliable facts.

Although Henry is responsible for providing his characters with names that have mythical associations, the events of his ballplayers' lives are determined by the 216 numerical combinations that exist in the rolls of three dice. Charts containing the actions that correspond to the numbers on the dice determine the behavior of each player. The familiar events of baseball fill most of the charts, but there are a considerable number of charts that determine the players' personal histories, their age, time as an active player, and death, for example. An "Extraordinary Occurrences Chart" covers unusual rolls of the dice, such as when the same number on each die appears through three consecutive throws. These events range from an exposed scandal to a player fatality.

Recording the events determined by the numbers on the dice, Henry, like Ralph Himebaugh, the numerologist in *The Origin of the Brunists*, discovers patterns in his tabulations that can be molded to fit his fantasies. In spite of the exciting coincidences and patterns of meaning they inspire, however, Henry eventually grows tired of the routine established by the constant recording of statistics. Nevertheless, he is loyal to his creation and keeps his records up to date. While the appearance of Damon Rutherford redeems Henry's waning interest in the game, the promise of a new era for the Universal Baseball Association is canceled by a roll of the dice that the "Extraordinary Occurrences Chart" determines is fatal to the Christ-figure. His patterns and hopes destroyed by the numbers in which he placed so much confidence, Henry is overwhelmed by his losses as he contemplates a future of confusion and emptiness.

Listening to Purcell's funeral march with Lou Engel, Henry imagines Rag Rooney leading a number of mourners in what sounds like a strange mixture of laughter and tears: "Rooney is giggling. Giggling hysterically. It infects them all. . . . Tee hee hee hee hee hee, boo hoo hoo hoo, tee hee hee hee, boo hoo hoo hoo . . . oops! the body bounces out! they pop it in again! out! in! it's one-old-cat, boys, with the earthly remains" (*UBA*, p. 92). Coover explains the meaning of the preceding quotation: "I hit on some very good ancient works full of lore. I . . . found a lot of good Aramaic and Hebrew words I was able to make puns of; for example: the words for 'confusion' and 'emptiness,' *tohu* and *bohu*, enter into the novel's funeral scene . . ." (Gado, p. 149). That Coover's puns may escape many of his readers "doesn't matter to me. I don't anticipate people seeing these things; what matters is that it was generative for me. The story I had in mind became richer. I would have had a funeral scene in any case, but now what it is really about is an evolution from the structural idea" (Gado, p. 149). The element of design notwithstanding, Barney Bancroft expresses a more catholic interpretation of the funeral march: "Funny thing about real gloom, . . . it had a giddy core. Made hard things soft, silly things true, grim things comic" (*UBA*, p. 95). Explaining the reasons behind the tone he has adopted in all of his works, Coover concurs: "I tend to think of tragedy as a kind of adolescent response to the universe—the higher truth is a comic response . . . there *is* a kind of humor extremity which is even more mature than the tragic response. Now that may seem in fact tragic. Thus some of the great ironic, comic fiction can nevertheless be equal to the same kind of strange emotion you get out of tragedy because your emotions can be mixed. And there's nothing wrong with an adolescent response; it's also real. . . . I don't think, barring a kind of regression of some sort, that we will ever have a time when tragedy will be *the* meaningful, full response to the universe" (Hertzel, p. 28).

After Rutherford's death, the association begins to deteriorate, and so does Henry. He drinks too much, does not sleep enough, fails to show up in time for work, makes a fool out of himself in front of Hettie and Lou Engel, and loses his job.

Torn between ridding himself of the game and being responsible to his creation, Henry reflects a parallel not only to God and his role of responsibility in the universe but also the fiction maker and his works. In each of these situations, the created works assume a status of their own that lies beyond their inventors' control, yet the created are still able to make demands on their makers. Interestingly, these demands of the created emphasize rather than lessen their makers dependency on their inventions. Like the Brunists, the ballplayers develop powers that make their dissolution difficult. The harder Henry tries to revenge Damon's death by destroying Jock Casey without disrupting the laws of his universe, for example, the more invincible does the pitcher become.

In his attempt to destroy Casey, Henry neglects his records, fails to log entries in "the Book," loses track of who is hitting and who is not, does not know if any pitchers are exceeding the legal limit of innings pitched, and no longer cares who wins the pennant. In short, he becomes as unaccountable to the game's history as he has been to the work assigned him by his employer.

In "The Tinkerer," a poem in which an inventor creates a human life and then refuses to be responsible for his creation's uncontrolled behavior, Coover presents a sentiment that is similar to Henry's.

he took a chance and invented mind
set it walking around jumping up and down seeing what it would do
if it could cut corners take steep hills how long before it ran
   down
not long and it was stiff and jerky at first cutting corners that
   weren't there and circling right into heavy traffic
. . . probably ought to shitcan this one he thought . . .
yet . . .
there was something engaging about it something that made him keep
   watching . . .

so he waited for it to run down screwed in number data recall concept
projection syntax wonder crossed a few wires and wound it up
   again . . .
but
the results were much the same except that now it *ran* at the
   walls *charged*
the traffic . . .
too late he realized that what he'd invented was not mind but
   love and now
he'd gone and blown it . . .
he tried to get ahold of his invention take all that junk out but
it was running amok
I'M NOT RESPONSIBLE! he cried . . .[10]

One night, when Lou Engel arrives at Henry's apartment with
a pizza, the proprietor serves beer and invites his friend to
participate in a game of paper baseball. Once again, Henry stacks
the odds against Jock Casey and his team, but Lou, who is
managing them against all logic, leads the Knicks over whatever
obstacles are in their way. Henry's team has its moments, but its
manager is ultimately disappointed when the opportunity for a
roll of sixes, which would necessitate a referral to the "Special
Stress Chart," evades him. Excited by the fortune that has
frustrated Henry, Lou accidentally spills his beer on everything
in sight: charts, scoresheets, logbooks, rosters, and records.
Furious over what Lou has done, Henry banishes his friend from
the apartment. Returning to the game, Henry, "almost ins-
tinctively" turns over the die reading "2" in order to complete a
6-6-6 throw. The game now having been moved to the
"Extraordinary Occurrences Chart," Henry discovers that
another roll of 6-6-6, the number of the beast in "Revelations"
and that of the anti-Christ in *The Omen*, would kill Jock Casey.
"Now, stop and think, he cautioned himself. Do you really *want*
to save it? Wouldn't it be better just to drop it now, . . . go on to
something else . . . if you killed that boy out there, then you
couldn't quit, could you? No, that's a real committment, you'd be
hung up for good, they wouldn't *let* you go" (*UBA*, p. 201).
   Henry's decision is not an easy one. To commit himself to the
fiction he has created would be a violation of all the rules he has
established for his universe. To kill Casey would, in the words of
Jackson Cope, substitute "sacrifice for chance, commitment for
causality, predestination for percentages.[11] Resolving to be

accountable to his fiction in a way that he has never been to his friends or work, Henry "picked up the dice, shook them. 'I'm sorry, boy,' he whispered, and then, holding the dice in his left palm, he set them down carefully with his right. One by one. Six. Six. Six (*UBA*, p. 202).

Although Henry's decision is a difficult one, it is not surprising. The creator began his day by banishing Hettie from his Eden for not playing by the rules of his game. Having hurt Henry's feelings by making innocent fun of the baseball game, Hettie tries to apologize, but receives only her pitcher's money and the open door to his apartment in response. That night, Henry casts from his paradise his only other friend, Lou Engel, whose name is a shortened version of Lucifer, the fallen angel. Having repaired the damage of the flood which covered his universe, Henry, as his creator in the Old Testament did before him, decides not to destroy or ignore his creation, but rather to commit himself more fully to it through the atonement of a human sacrifice. Interestingly, Jock Casey's death not only redeems his brothers in the association, as Christ's death atoned for the sins of his fellow man, but he saves Henry, his creator, from turning his back on his fiction and participating in the real world of Lou Engel. Vomiting a rainbow of pizza over his altered universe, Henry provides his ballplayers with a sign of the covenant he has made with them.

As he has done in many of his earlier works, Coover establishes a pattern familiar to his readers, then shifts his allegory in order to make an ironic comment about his readers' conventional perspectives. In *The Origin of the Brunists,* Coover refocused his readers' orientation from Marcella Bruno as the Brunists' sacrificial figure to Tiger Miller; in *The Universal Baseball Association, Inc.,* Coover seduces his readers into viewing Damon as the redemptive Christ-figure, then replaces him with Jock Casey. In that same way that Tiger Miller went from the Brunists' Judas to their Jesus, so too does Jock Casey develop from an anti-Christ at the novel's beginning to the association's savior at its end. Speaking of the patterns he developed in *The Universal Baseball Association, Inc.,* Coover says, "Even though the structure is not profoundly meaningful in itself, I love to use it. This has been the case ever since the earliest things I wrote when I made an arbitrary commitment to design. The reason is not that I have some notion of an underlying ideal order which fiction imitates, but a delight with the rich ironic possibilities that the use of structure affords. Any idea, even one which on the surface doesn't seem very interesting, fitted with a perfect structure, can blossom into something that even I did not suspect was there originally. Engaging in that process of discovery is the excitement of making fiction.

"The Henry book came into being for me when I found a simple structural key to the metaphor of a man throwing dice for a baseball game he has made up. It suddenly occurred to me to use Genesis I.1 to II.3—seven chapters corresponding to the seven days of creation—and this in turn naturally implied an eighth, the apocalyptic day. Having decided on this basic plan, I read a lot of exegetical works on that part of the Bible in order to find out as much as I could which would reinforce and lend meaning to the division into parts" (Gado, pp. 148-49).

After Henry's interference in the workings of the association, the game, as Chancellor McCaffree predicted, becomes reduced to a form without substance. Women and politics and the past supersede in importance the great American game. Nevertheless, a sense of order exists that was absent in the association's early days. Barney Bancroft is writing a league history called *The UBA in Balance*. As its title suggests, the league has reached a sense of equilibrium; yet, at the same time, it is moving forward. Barney has discovered that perfection, like writing, is a process. The nature of this transformation, Barney explains, is from "individualism and egocentrism" to "a moral and philosophical concern with the very nature of man and society" (*UBA*, pp. 216-17). Coover's book, then, might very well serve as a model for Bancroft's: "The world itself being a construct of fictions," says Henry's creator, "I believe the fiction-maker's function is to furnish better fictions with which we can re-form our notions of things. Yet there is a paradox in that very activity. In order to accomplish his ends, the writer, by the nature of his profession, must himself withdraw entirely. You could say I wrote the baseball book not for baseball buffs or even for theologians but for other writers" (Gado, pp. 149-50). Unfortunately for Coover, the metaphor through which he hopes to re-form his fellow writers' "notions of things" has proven to be unsatisfactory: "It would be marvelous to find the perfect, natural, popular image to which everyone could relate. It would be ideal to have the audience feel it, get into it so that things would happen to them without their even being aware it's happening to them, and absorb through the back door the history and culture they didn't have before. Unfortunately, metaphors are seldom that productive. Most prove to be much more esoteric than you first thought.

"Take the baseball image: the average American male knows baseball and can follow a character playing a baseball parlor game. Even that it is a parlor game presents no problem. So it is very useful for most readers, especially for the poorer ones, not accustomed to that kind of fiction, who read somewhere it is a good book, pick it up, and get all the way through to the end. They can say, 'Gee, I was able to read a good book'; maybe, they will go on to read another good book and see if it happens a second time. Nevertheless, for most women it's a rather dull approach to a novel. And Europeans don't understand it at all: when it was published in England, no one knew what to make of it, even though I supplied a glossary" (Gado, p. 158).

One hundred association years after the deaths of Damon Rutherford and Jock Casey, Henry has withdrawn totally from what Barney Bancroft calls "real time" into "significant time" (*UBA,* p. 217). Henry's presence is seen through all of the players' attempts to cope with life. Not surprisingly, these attempts reflect much of Henry's confusion. Many are philosophically and theologically skeptical; a book called *The Doubter* is being passed around by the players. Others drink too much, search for patterns in the random events of the association, become reborn as Caseyites, or try to find truth in the league's history. The characters most like Henry, however, are Paul Trench and Royce Ingram, sons of two famous Hall of Famers. Paul's epiphany and transformation through Royce's support is the last event of the novel and seen through their eyes. Indeed, Paul's apprehension about the game reflects more accurately than the thoughts of any other player the dreams, fears, and guilt of Henry, while Royce's confidence in the game, like Henry's, exceeds all others.

The major event of the apocalyptic chapter, in which the "real" Henry has disappeared entirely, is the ritual performance of "Damonsday," a sort of passion play in which the year's current rookies commemorate the death of Damon Rutherford and the sacrifice of Jock Casey. This "baseballmass" continues the religious motifs established in the book's previous seven chapters and emphasizes Henry's belief in the ballpark as a sort of American house of worship. Many of the players, however, feel that "Damonsday" is a meaningless exercise. Some doubt if Rutherford or Casey ever existed. Nevertheless, Henry continues to replay the events of Rutherford's and Casey's deaths as he reinforces his commitment to the association and perhaps assuages the guilt he feels for having interfered in the league's events. Through Paul Trench and Royce Ingram, then, Henry participates significantly in the process of transformation described by Barney Bancroft. What counts for Henry is that he loves his game; it is his life force. No longer the befuddled Jahweh that resembles Happy Bottom's Judge in *The Origin of the Brunists,* Henry knows that conflicts within the association are a part of the process toward unreachable perfection and consequently irrelevant; "it doesn't matter that he's going to die, all that counts is that he is *here* and here's The Man and here's the boys and there's the crowd, the sun, the noise" (*UBA,* p. 242).

Henry's final position in the novel, which, like Happy Bottom's "Black Hand" messages, proclaims the importance of the immediate and everyday is a life-affirming response to the rat race, his employer, and what he reads in the newspapers. Nevertheless, the fact that Henry's affirmation is purely fictional has led some critics to question its quality. Leo Hertzel, for example, believes that "the game has come to have no meaning for Waugh any more. He is still there, shadowy, unreliable, shaking the dice, but the joy is gone. Perhaps he will close down the circuit soon, find another hobby. This one hasn't been too successful. . . . The re-enacting of the senseless death of Damon Rutherford is as meaningless as the Brunists' seeking signs."[12] Frank Shelton, on the other hand, believes that the novel does not justify Hertzel's conclusion:

Destroying Jock Casey involved commitment and affirmation on Henry's part, which he referred to earlier when he thought: "either something happened—something in short *remedial*—or into the garbage bag with the whole works" [*UBA,* pp. 127—28]. Any speculation about where Henry is or what his state of mind would be useless, just as, finally, any speculation about the existence of power behind the dice is beside the point. We are led to these possibilities but are convinced by the novel that the problem is insoluble and does not matter, for the world Henry created remains alive. That the Damonsday ritual and the myths it embodies are perhaps without ultimate meaning does not imply that they have no useful function.

Indeed, Coover's novel has brought form to experience, as baseball and the rituals which have arisen from it have done. . . . Reality lies not simply in the ritual itself but both in it and independent of it.[13]

Judith Wood Angelius disagrees. Henry's presence at the end of the novel is central to its theme:

The irony that Henry savored when he killed Jock Casey, ironically favors his own end. For while the reality of the living moment is exalted at the conclusion of the novel, Henry has lost touch with the real world altogether. Although he created the Universal Baseball Association in an attempt to counterbalance the imprisoning skyscrapers, the whorehouse of war, and the lunacy around him, he is now more imprisoned than ever. . . . This irony points to the tragedy underlying the comic ending of the novel, and adds dimension to a resolution that, otherwise, would be pat and simplistic. . . . Now, more than ever, Henry is up against the wall. He never found the exit he so desperately wanted. . . . Ironically, Henry . . . ends up trapped in the very role he tried to escape.[14]

Jackson I. Cope's argument counters Angelius's. Through fiction and remythification, he says, "Robert Coover converts the dark parable of our insane culture into an affirmation that salvation is still possible through the daemonic sense of play with which he is so richly endowed."[15] Clarifying Cope's point about remythification and responding to Shelton's view that "any speculation about the existence of power behind the dice is beside the point," Arlen J. Hansen writes:

Einstein fictionalized quantum mechanics as God playing dice with the universe. As long as we accept this conception we are disposed to doubting and disproving the veracity of quantum theory. Once we remind ourselves that Einstein's is only one fictive conception, we might feel free to re-mythify and, thus, subsequently to entertain another, perhaps more helpful fiction. Einstein's conception points up the chanciness implicit in the uncertainty principle. . . . Einstein's conceptual version might well be re-mythified in the equally imagistic language of Sophocles: "The dice of Zeus ever fall aright" (Fragment 763). Perhaps the dynamics and nature of atomic phenomena do dispose us toward thinking in terms of God and dice. If so, the new fiction might emphasize (for the time being at least) that the dice of God are governed by deterministic and probalistic laws embedded in quantum theory: God *does* play dice with the universe, but the dice are loaded.[16]

Damon's final words in the novel, spoken through Royce Ingram, have often been cited as Coover's most likely response to the confusion outlined above: " 'It's not a trial,' says Damon, glove tucked in his armpit, hands working the ball. Behind him, he knows, Scot Batkin, the batter, is moving toward the plate. 'It's not even a lesson. It's just what is' " (*UBA*, p. 242). Nevertheless, Coover's fiction eludes even this simple perspective. Life is not merely a game without any messages; it is a game that man has invented to help him order and comprehend the random events of the universe. He needs the game he has created. Speaking of Sandy Shaw's folksongs and the ball players gathering together after Damon's funeral, Henry says, "Men needed these rituals, after all, that was part of the truth, too, and certainly the Association benefited from them. Men's minds being what they generally were, it was the only way to get to most of them . . ." (*UBA*, p. 103). Though men need myths, however, they do not have to believe in them. The disservice of the myths man invents and attaches to life, says Coover through the persona of Henry, is their blocking of his perception of the truth, namely, the conscious recognition of his dogmas' fictional nature. As with so many people, Henry has lost touch with his real self through his belief in the fiction he has created. Ironically, Henry achieves affirmation by withdrawing completely into the personae of his players because he sees the game as it "really" is: "There were patterns, but they were shifting and ambiguous and you had a lot of room inside them. Secondly, that the game on his table was not a message, but an event . . ." (*UBA*, p. 143). In other words, Henry sees the game through the perspective that Coover wishes his readers would envision life. Because Henry's vision is a game, however, his affirmation is limited. Unfortunately, he has transformed his life into a fiction rather than recognizing, accepting, and playing the real game that people call "life."

III   *"McDuff on the Mound"*

"McDuff on the Mound," the story of "Casey at the Bat" told from the pitcher's point of view, reads as if Coover, having demythified religion and history, decided to provide sports with the same service. Except for the Disney-like pratfalls of some of its characters, however, and the comment that every endeavor requires great effort and is usually accompanied by pain, the story repeats many of Coover's established themes, the most important of which is the necessity of man's recognizing his culture's fictional nature and freeing himself, aesthetically and ideologically, from its conventional doctrines.

When, in the bottom of the ninth with two outs and his team ahead by two runs, he gives up a bloop single to Fat Flynn, McDuff suspects that he is about to play a role in a familiar pattern of events:

McDuff, a practical man with both feet on the ground, had always tried to figure the odds, and that's where he'd gone wrong. But would things have been different if Cooney and Burroughs had hit him? Not substantially maybe, there'd still be much the same situation and Casey yet to face. But the stage wouldn't have been just right, and maybe, because of that, he'd have got out of it. (*MM*. p. 112)[17]

In the batter's box, Blake "The Cake," tries to knock the dirt out of his cleats, but each time he lifts his foot, he loses his balance and falls. Lying on the ground, he manages a healthy swing of his bat but hits his foot. Picking up his bat, which has been broken into two sections, the largest of which hangs like a big splinter from its handle, Blake takes a warm-up swing and knocks himself out with the dangling end of the bat. The reader's response, which is pretty much the same as if he was watching the Walt Disney "Goofy" cartoon Coover is re—creating, becomes slightly more serious when Blake and the umpire begin switching hats. Later, when Blake and Flynn begin exchanging clothes with each other and McDuff, the reader recognizes a stunt that has been played by Stan Laurel, Oliver Hardy, Buster Keaton, Charlie Chaplin, Samuel Beckett's clowns, and a host of others. Like his forerunners, Coover is telling his readers that even the most modest of life's accomplishments require pain and effort. Struggling is one thing all men have in common.

When Blake finally gets a hit with a bat that is so heavy he has to hold it up with his head, McDuff is ready for the showers, but, as Henry Waugh and Sycamore Flynn discovered in a similar situation in *The Universal Baseball Association, Inc.*, he cannot quit. While Fat Flynn and Turkey Blake act out hackneyed vaudeville routines on the basepaths, McDuff grows increasingly more frustrated and depressed over the winning home run he knows Casey is going to hit. As the team's outfielders search for the ball Blake's "swing" took the cover off of, McDuff's battery-mate, Gus, argues with the game's umpire over a technical ruling. The umpire believes that Blake's Texas leaguer is an automatic home run, but Gus asserts that since Mudville Field has no official limits, there can be no automatic homers. In light of the ideas he has expressed in his prologue to "Seven Exemplary Fictions" and the treatment he has given these themes in other works, Coover's allegory is obvious. Fiction, like Mudville Field, has no limits; therefore, it has no automatic rules. Consulting his rule book, the umpire sees that Gus is right: "He read it aloud: 'Mudville's field is open-ended. Nothing is automatic here, in spite of appearances. A ball driven even unto Gehenna is not necessarily a homerun. In short, anything can happen in Mudville, even though most things are highly improbable. Blake, for example, has never had a hit, nor has Casey yet struck out'" (*MM*, p. 116).

Finally, McDuff's shortstop finds the ball and, with the help of Blake's and Flynn's inept base-running, prevents two runs from scoring. There is a glimmer of hope in the pitcher's eye, but he represses it and faces the inevitable. At bat is the hometown favorite, Casey. A home run will win the game for Mudville. As it was for Henry Waugh the night Lou Engel came over to play paper baseball, the stage has been set against all that is reasonable.

Trying to calm his pitcher down, Gus walks to the mound to have a talk with him. Through the catcher's advice and support, the pitcher outgrows some of his own naiveté. Forgetting about the stage and the patterns that have been forming on it, McDuff throws his first pitch right down the pipeline but a little to the outside to give Casey plenty of room to swing. Strike one. The crowd, which resembles the terrifying audience of "Panel Game," screams viciously, but a gesture from Casey calms them down. McDuff repeats his pitch; the umpire, the crowd, and Casey repeat themselves. Having delivered two pitches he would be embarrassed to throw in batting practice, McDuff realizes that Casey is more myth than substance. The pressure now off of him and onto Casey makes McDuff giggle. Echoing Barney Bancroft of *The Universal Baseball Association, Inc.*, the narrator says, ". . . Now that everybody else had got serious, McDuff suddenly found it was all just a gas. . . . He giggled furtively: there's always something richly ludicrous about extremity" (*MM*, p. 119). Sending his third pitch right down the middle of the plate, McDuff watches Casey's swing split the air with a thunderous roar. Myths can make a powerful noise, but their substance is less than air and man is better off not believing in them.

Ironically, the myth of the local hero hitting the winning home run in the bottom of the ninth had already been deflated by the author of "Casey at the Bat" before Coover wrote "McDuff on the Mound." Casey strikes out in the poem just as he does in Coover's story. Consequently, Coover's failure to shift the patterns of his readers' expectations as he has done in other stories is disappointing and uncharacteristic of him. Neverthe-less, "McDuff on the Mound" effectively lampoons the myth of mighty Casey and makes a case for the liberation of the mind from conventional molds. As in the Donald Warren stories, "The Square-Shooter and the Saint" and "Dinner with the King of England," however, Coover here also argues intelligently against the idea that innocence is an attractive quality. Had McDuff retained his naive awe of Casey, he would never have struck him out and would never have become famous through the poem and short story. The limitations of innocence, however, go beyond DonaldWarren's experiences in Jerusalem and London and McDuff's resistance to recognizing the fictional nature of myth. In *The Universal Baseball Association, Inc.*, Henry's innocence inflicts serious psychological damage upon him. Throughout the book, Henry is plagued by the presence of a young boy, a lonely reminder of his innocence that he hopes to protect through a variety of psychic projections. When Damon dies, Henry imagines the hysterical reaction of the Poineers' fans and the image of a boy standing alone in the crowd. "Who was that boy?" he asks (*UBA*, p. 57). The reader remembers him as the youngster to whom Damon Rutherford tossed a baseball on the day he pitched a perfect game. At Damon's funeral, the boy again appears: ". . . Suddenly, the thin voice of a small boy cried out, a boy in terror, boy gripping a baseball, gift of the slain giant, boys all, hurt, terrified, the emptiness, the confusion" (*UBA*, p. 90). One hundred years after Damon's death, the boy in Henry is still present: "Yes, my God, *that same kid*! Who the hell are you, he wants to ask, but something holds him back" (*UBA*, p. 228). The haunting child is the innocence that Henry tries to protect from reality. It is the boy in him that needs to believe in myths, heroes, and a son of his own, and leads him to create the dangerous escape that eventually imprisons him.

"Blackdamp," *The Origin of the Brunists,* "The Second Son," *The Universal Baseball Association, Inc., J. Henry Waugh, Prop.,* and "McDuff on the Mound" have much to say against man's tendency to try to order his experience and find patterns of meaning in the order he has fictionalized. Much in life is left to chance, says Coover, but his works also suggest that if man is willing to play the game of life with his eyes open, that is, with intelligence, shrewdness, genuine emotion, and an uncompromising desire for quality, he can load the dice in his favor and broaden the breadth and depth of his consciousness all the way to Gehenny!

CHAPTER 3

More Exemplary Fictions

I Pricksongs and Descants

"**M**Y FIRST THOUGHT was to publish a book of exemplary fictions. I had about forty stories I would have included: some of which were realistic or naturalistic—similar to Cervantes's range in his exemplary novellas. But one doesn't as a rule publish a book of stories early in a career, I was told, so for quite a while I couldn't bring it out. Then, later, when the time was ripe, there was only a handful of the stories I still wanted to keep.[1] Realizing I would have to write more, I tried to come up with another organizing principle that would enable me to use some of the stuff I already had and to produce a book that had a beginning, a middle, and an end.

"A lot of *Pricksongs* I wrote not knowing at all what I was doing, not having a clue as to why I felt it was necessary to write this kind of story. It was hit or miss. The earliest piece in the collection, 'The Panel Game,' represents the turning point for me; it was written in 1957. The second oldest, 'The Marker,' I did in 1960; the next, in 1962. The jumps mean that a large number of fictions haven't been included.[2] Some things would seem very necessary, but after I would start writing them, they seldom seemed worth the effort; they were strange, incomplete things, often very shallow. A *few* of them did work, but I didn't know why; I was going on instinct you see.

"Well I decided that, instinct being very unreliable, I should try to understand, to go deeper into the mechanics of the narrative form. I turned to the ancient fictions to research what had already been done and also to see what new ideas they might engender. The *Arabian Nights,* I discovered, was a gold mine of formal possibilities—and although I made specific use of none,

79

they provided a context which made what I was writing seem real.

"Going back to Ovid produced a similar response. The Ovidian stories all concern transformation; now that is not a startlingly new subject—after all, fairy tales, animal fables, and the like, deal with it—but I suddenly realized that the basic, constant struggle for all of us is against metamorphosis, against giving in to the inevitability of the process. Encountering in Ovid the same agon that underlay my own writing was liberating; I realized that what I was already doing was not only possible but essential" (Gado, pp. 151-52).

As with his earliest collections of stories, "Seven Exemplary Fictions" and "The Sentient Lens," the works that Coover wrote after *The Origin of the Brunists* can be divided roughly into two categories: the first concerns the retelling of familiar stories from a new perspective; the second involves stories that emphasize the variety of technical possibilities available when literature is free from conventional narrative forms. Before the publication of *The Origin of the Brunists,* Coover limited his reinterpretation of familiar narratives to biblical stories. His later retellings, however, explore the infrequently visited regions of fairy tales and, at the same time, emphasize the infinite number of ways they can be related. William Gass explains the effect of Coover's process on the reader this way: "Just like the figures in old fairy tales, we are constantly coming to forks in the road (always fateful), except here we take all of them, and our simultaneous journeys are simultaneous stories, yet in different genres, sometimes different styles, as if fantasy, romance and reality, nightmare and daydream, were fingers on the same hand."[3] The stories in *Pricksongs and Descants* that are not derivative of fairy tales also stress Coover's insistence on the multiple possibilities of fiction. The nature of reality, he seems to be saying, is so complex that any single way of interpreting it must necessarily be false. Hence, the problem of nature's multiplicity becomes, for Coover, its own solution. For literature to truly represent nature, it must be as variable as nature itself. To accomplish this end, Coover sets about to dismantle the arbitrary set of narrative conventions that he has inherited from tradition. Speaking about the necessity of recognizing new perspectives, Coover says, "In part because individual human existence is so brief, in part because each single instant of the world is so impossibly complex, we cannot accumulate all the data needed for a complete, objective statement. To hope to behave as though this were possible is to invite paralysis through crushing despair. And so we fabricate; we invent constellations that permit an illusion of order to enable us to get from here to there. And we devise short cuts—ways of thinking without thinking through: code words that are in themselves a form of mythopoeia. Thus, in a sense, we are all creating fictions all the time, out of necessity. We constantly test them against the experience of life. Some continue to be functional; we are content to let them be rather than try to analyze them and, in the process, forget something else that is even more important. Others outlive their usefulness. They disturb life in some unnecessary way, and so it becomes necessary to break them up and perhaps change their force" (Gado, p. 152).

Although critics have labeled Coover's pricksongs and descants anything from Cubist structures to montages and solitaires, the technique employed in elucidating the importance of fictional variety is pretty much the same for each short story. Coover begins each of the stories in this collection with elements that are familiar to his readers. The style of Coover's writing may be realistic, for example, or the opening lines may contain recognizable allusions to the popular culture. As soon as his readers become comfortable with what they think they know, however, Coover pulls the rug out from under them and sets a number of other plot lines in motion. These additional plots, often containing narrative voices of their own, prevent the reader from determining which perspective is the most reliable. By telling his stories from a variety of viewpoints, Coover confuses his reader by rendering him incapable of distinguishing between what occurs in people's minds and what is really happening. Unlike J. Henry Waugh, who became imprisoned in the Universal Baseball Association that he invented, however, the narrators of *Pricksongs and Descants* are very much aware of their constructs' artificial nature and invite the reader to participate in their "elaborate game, embellished with masks and poetry, a marshalling of legendary doves and herbs (*PD*, p. 18).[4] The result, according to William Gass, "is a book of virtuoso exercises: alert, self-conscious, instructional, and show off."[5] Gass's praise notwithstanding, *Pricksongs and Descants* reflects more than Coover's arbitrary commitment to design: "All of us today are keenly aware that we are undergoing a radical shift in sensibilities. We are no longer convinced of the *nature* of things, of design as justification. Everything seems itself random. (The early existentialists were leading us this way; since then, we have seen the breakdown of religious structures and of many of the principles of the Enlightenment which have supported our institutions.) Under these conditions of arbitrariness, the artistic impulse is directed toward putting the random parts together in any order which provides a pattern for living" (Gado, p. 153).

"The Door: A Prologue of Sorts" introduces the stories collected in *Pricksongs and Descants* in the sense that Coover invites his readers to enter the door he has opened unto new fictional worlds. In addition to reinterpreting "Jack and the Beanstalk," "Beauty and the Beast," and "Little Red Riding Hood" through the voices of three narrators, "The Door" comments on the individual's initiation into adult realities and the art of creating fiction. Two of the new perspectives in the story, that of the adult Jack and Granny, are told retrospectively. Recalling their own transitions to maturity, they ponder the possibilities awaiting Little Red Riding Hood. They remember having become disillusioned by a world with which their inherited traditions had not prepared them to cope. They have become bitter with the lies they were told when they were too young to be skeptical. Consequently, they have not passed on the fairy tales they learned as children to Little Red Riding Hood but neither have they prepared her for the reality she is about to discover.

The first of these three stories within a story is Jack's. Now a giant himself, Jack remembers his adventures as a youth, but life has not turned out the way the boy with the golden goose expected. To be a man in the adult world means hard work and mating with women who grow old. Having been deceived by those who painted a picture of life that was exceeded by his vision of it, Jack has not related his culture's lies to Little Red Riding Hood. Nevertheless, his interest in her happiness as well as his concern that she may someday fear and hate prevent Jack from being honest. Having taught Little Red Riding Hood to enjoy life but having simultaneously failed to prepare her for it, Jack feels guilty for the false expectations he has nurtured and the despair he knows they will exacerbate.

At this point, Little Red Riding Hood's grandmother, in a

Joycean style characteristic of "The Brother," narrates the story of "Beauty and the Beast" from her present perspective. Unfortunately for Granny, the Beast, though she loved him, never metamorphosed into the prince her fairy tales had promised. Granny's disillusionment, of course, is part of the maturation process, and, like Jack, she is bitter. Waiting for Little Red Riding Hood to come with her basket of goodies, pun intended, Granny complains:

oh I know why she's late you warn her and it does no good I know who's got her giddy ear with his old death-cunt-and-prick songs haven't I heard them all my God and smelt his hot breath in the singin? . . . bit of new fuzz on her pubes and juice in the little bubbies and off she prances into that world of hers that ain't got forests nor prodigies a dippy smile on her face and her skirts up around her ears well well . . . let her go tippy-toin through the flux and tedium and trip on her dropped drawers a few times and see if she don't come runnin back to old Granny. . . . (*PD*, pp. 15-16)

In addition to presenting a viewpoint of the world that combines beauty with terror, the book's title contains an obvious musical allusion: "In a way, the title is redundant because a pricksong is a descant. There is a shade of difference, however. 'Pricksong' derives from the physical manner in which the song was printed—the notes were literally pricked out; 'descant' refers to the form of music in which there is a *cantus firmus*, a basic line, and variations that the other voices play against it. The early descants, being improvisations, were unwritten; when they began writing them the idea of a counterpoint, of a full, beautiful harmony emerged.

"Of course, there is also the obvious sexual suggestion. In this connection, I thought of the descants as feminine decoration around the pricking of the basic line. Thus: the masculine thrust of narrative and the lyrical play around it.

"The terms were useful to me because they were pre-Enlightenment, pre-Monteverdian, and so a part of the art forms that have been shunted aside by the developments of the last three hundred years. The choice of the title had to do with my decision to focus on Cervantes as a turning point" (Gado, pp. 150-51).

Little Red Riding Hood, as might be expected, is both curious and anxious about her position at the threshhold of maturity. The door, of course, represents the girl's passage into adulthood and the new perspectives she will acquire, but it also symbolizes the path through which Coover's creative readers will be able to relinquish their "adolescent thought-modes" and develop an interest in fictional variety and ambiguity.

In addition to retelling the story of "Hansel and Gretel" from the perspective of the father, "The Gingerbread House" presents a narrative technique that has become increasingly indentified with Coover. Instead of telling the story in a style that is familiar to his readers, Coover creates forty-two short sections, each one presenting a self-contained image. Like pearls on a necklace, they join together to create a narrative that, by the nature of its construction, is fragmented and connected rather than related. This technique emphasizes the story's ambiguity and encourages Coover's readers to consider a variety of conclusions and interpretations. To insure uncertainty in the resolution-oriented minds of his readers, Coover punctuates his fragmented images with words such as "perhaps," "as if," and "seems." Furthermore, his placing a description of the sleeping Hansel and Gretel toward the end of the story implies that the realistic events of the tale may be those of a dream. Finally, Coover disrupts his readers' conventional approaches to literature in general by developing a pattern of color and floral images that bear no relation to the story. What meaningful patterns the author does create stem from additions that, when blended with elements from the traditional story, invites the reader to discover previously unconsidered values in a tale he thinks he has outgrown.

"The Gingerbread House" begins with the father leading his two children into the woods. Although the children are unnamed, the boy's furtive dropping of breadcrumbs along the trail they make signal the story's origin. By omitting everything in the Grimm brothers' tale that precedes the journey described in the reinterpretation, however, Coover seduces his readers into completing what the fragmented story leaves out of the original tale. As a result, the reader develops certain patterns in his mind that Coover can, somewhat unfairly, manipulate. For example, the Grimm brothers' tale focuses attention on children who interpret their parents' designs to help them become independent as a form of rejection and, consequently, they seek reunion. The witch, whom the children meet, becomes their mother substitute. However, when Hansel and Gretel discover that to be dependent on the female figure means that they must forfeit their identities, they overthrow the witch and attain psychological independence. In "The Gingerbread House," on the other hand, Coover uses the materials of "Hansel and Gretel" to frustrate his readers' traditional interpretation of the story and introduces them to another view of initiation into the adult world. By having his fiction end with Hansel and Gretel about to enter the witch's cottage instead of being reunited with their father and by endowing his tale with a series of sexual images that the Grimm brothers never considered, Coover changes the emphasis of psychological independence in the story to initiation. In fact, "The Gingerbread House" is more closely aligned with "The Door" than "Hansel and Gretel."

The father in "The Gingerbread House" is like Jack in "The Door." His life has not turned out to be what his parents' fairy tales have led him to expect in life. Consequently, he wants to keep his children as children. He tells them a bedtime story that delays for a short time their entering the Gingerbread House, which, of course, will lead to other threshholds that must be crossed before adulthood can be achieved. As in Coover's retelling of "Little Red Riding Hood," the first door through which the children must pass is sexual. Not only the door, but many of the images that precede the appearance of the witch's house are presented in sexual terms: the boy's hand and wrist thrust from his outgrown jacket; the girl's basket is full to overflowing. The girl's reaction to the dead dove is particularly explicit: "She has thrust the dove protectively beneath her skirt, and sits, knees apart, leaning over it, weeping softly. The old man stoops down, lifts her bright orange apron, her skirt, her petticoats. . . . The dove is nested in her small round thighs" (*PD*, p. 67). Finally, the door to the Gingerbread House, which children enter but do not leave, is described in the same terms as the dove's heart, which the witch has extracted from the bird and uses as a sexual lure. The dove's heart "glitters like a . . . polished cherry, a brilliant, heart-shaped bloodstone. . . . The glowing heart pulses gently, evenly, excitingly" (*PD*, pp. 66–71). Similarly, the "door is shaped like a heart and is as red as a cherry, always half-open. . . . It is . . . blood-stone-red, . . . and pulsing softly, radiantly" (*PD*, pp. 68–75). Through his description of the dove and the door to the Gingerbread House,

Coover identifies the kind of initiation Hansel and Gretel will experience.

In his reinterpretation of "Little Red Riding Hood," Coover associates sex with violence. The beast lying within Jack "got ahold of him . . ." and Granny has "been split with the pain and terrible haste of his thick quick cock . . ." (*PD*, p. 15, 17). In "The Gingerbread House," Coover again associates sex with terror. The witch seduces the boy with a heart she has torn out of a dove. The boy and girl lick candy off of one another, but they also fight. The father lusts after the witch, but hypocritically slaps the boy for having the same desires. Perhaps because of instances such as these, the children, like Little Red Riding Hood, are apprehensive about their sexual awakening: "Oh, what a thing is that door! . . . Yes, marvelous! delicious! insuperable! but beyond: what is that sound of black rags flapping?" (*PD*, p. 75).

In light of Jack's disillusion, Granny's bitterness, and the father's fear for his children's welfare, Coover's unattractive portrayal of adulthood does not come as surprise to the reader. Though the state of maturity may seem at least sexually tantalizing it is a world where, according to Coover, evil is seldom overcome, innocent white doves have their hearts torn out, and good fairies are impotent. In the world of adults, the magic is real, the onimous fairy tales about uncertainty are true, and the beasts are genuine human essences that lie within all who inhabit this region. Nevertheless, the world of adult realities provides opportunities for adventure that childhood lacks. Removed from the protective, limited perspective their father has given them, the children as well as those readers who free themselves from the security of literary conventions are free to "complete the story with their own wishes, their own dreams" (*PD*, p. 69).

In his article "Robert Coover and the Hazards of Metafiction," Neil Schmitz claims that Coover's "The Door" and "The Gingerbread House" read as if they are

little more than adulterated versions of the TV cartoon, *Fractured Fairytales*. . . . When opened, the Door to the Gingerbread House reveals, not existential terrors, but the wizard/writer busily wrenching symbolic language into rearranged patterns. Coover's professed aim to conduct the reader away from 'mystification to clarification' is laboriously achieved in these tales. In brief, it is only a different kind of effect that Coover strives to produce in his fiction by deconstructing the 'familiar form.' The result is not a transcendence of that form, but rather a transposition of its elements.[6]

Certainly, there is some truth to Schmitz's observation. Coover's retellings of "Little Red Riding Hood" and "Hansel and Gretel," like the *Fractured Fairytales*, depend upon an audience whose perception of the original stories enables them to understand the comment the satiric version is making. However, Coover's representations of innocence lost, man's sexual awakenings, and the passage of children into adulthood go beyond the gently ironic parodies of the television cartoon. More than a display of technical wizardry, Coover's fairy tales provide their author with universally accepted metaphors through which he can effectively relate his ideas about fiction and the human condition.

"The Dead Queen," "Some Notes About Puff," and "Valley of the Fallen, 3 July" complete Coover's statement on the use of fairy tales. Though not included in the *Pricksongs and Descants* collection, "The Dead Queen" is similar to "The Door" and "The Gingerbread House" in that it calls to mind a familiar story, that of "Snow White and the Seven Dwarfs." The narrator, Prince Charming, begins his story at the funeral of the dead Queen, who was jealous of Snow White's beauty. He and his new bride are supposed to live happily ever after, but the Prince has his doubts. Snow White, in his eyes, seems to be "utterly heartless," though not malicious, "like a happy child at the circus, unaware of any skills or risks . . . she's suffered no losses, in fact that's just the trouble, that hymen can never be broken, not even by me. . . . This is her gift and her essence, and because of it, she can see neither fore nor aft, doesn't even know there is a mirror on the wall."[7] Reflecting upon the crimes the Queen committed against Snow White, Prince Charming wonders if the allegedly evil stepmother had been motivated to poison Snow White for reasons other than jealousy:

She'd sent that child of seven into the woods with a restless lech, and he'd brought her back a boar's heart, as though to say he repented of his irrational life and wished to die. But then, perhaps that had been what she wanted, perhaps she had ordered the boar's heart, or known anyway that would be the Hunter's instinct, or perhaps there had been no Hunter at all, perhaps it had been that master of disguises, the old Queen herself, it was possible, it was all possible. (pp. 308-309)

Pondering alternative versions to the traditional story sobers Prince Charming, who finds himself troubled by many things to which he had not given much thought: "the true meaning of my bride's name, her taste for luxury and collapse, the compulsions that had led me to the mountain . . . (pp. 307-308). Suddenly, it dawns on the Prince that the Queen might have been trying to save him from Snow White, break the pattern of the fairy tale, and free its characters from its traditional bonds. Believing that he retains the power that his fiction maker bestowed upon him for his own purposes, Prince Charming wrenches open the coffin, throws himself upon the Queen, and kisses her in the hope of restoring her to life. The Queen, however, does not return Prince Charming's kiss: "She stank and her blue mouth was cold and rubbery as a dead squid" (p. 313).

"Some Notes About Puff," a rewording of the folksong "Puff the Magic Dragon," is a work-in-progress that also focuses the reader's attention on the breaking of conventional patterns and on the number of possibilities available within any fiction. After recounting the familiar business about Jackie Paper, the cave, and Honah Lee, Puff wonders if the value attached to eating pearls is not a myth:

He eats them and they just pass through, untransfigured—well, of course, magic stones, ultimately unalterable and all that, but still, it's enough to make one doubt. Just as an experiment, or maybe out of some vague dissatisfaction with his career, Puff tries to reverse the process: suck them up his ass and spew them out his mouth. But it doesn't work, they just clog up there, give him sphincterache and an inflamed prostate. . . . He'd quit, but he's been sucking pearls for ages, and it'd be hard now to kick the habit.

As an example of some of the possibilities available to writers than can kick the habit of tradition, Coover presents a seemingly infinite list of the meanings Puff's pearl may contain.

THE PEARL: an emblem of beauty, of fidelity and humility, a sign of self-sacrifice and sorrow, of innocence, integrity, purity, rarity, tears, and vaginal dew, of virginity and wealth and wisdom. Powdered pearl in lemon juice cures lunacy, bellyache, and epilepsy. It is an attribute of moon goddesses, Christ, cows, pudenda, and the Virgin Mary, is used in all Eastern love potions and protects chastity in the West. Pigafetta, travelling with Magellan, reported that the king of Borneo dropped his pants and showed him two as large as goose eggs. The pearl is a Christian symbol of salvation and a particle of the consecrated eucharist wafer, a Chinese charm against fire, a Moslem condition of the hereafter: the faithful endure forever, encapsulated in pearls, each with his own exquisite virgin, Allah's wages to the orthodox. The Chinese in the sixth century also believed it rained pearls when dragons fought in the sky, but some beliefs are not true. We now know in fact that such storms are more often triggered by sudden eclipses in the erogenous zones of quasars. . . .[8]

Through the catalogue of metaphors that ends "Some Notes About Puff," Coover pleads for an open-ended system of writing that allows for an infinite number of fictional possibilities. Such a system, he believes, emphasizes the imaginative nature of fiction and resists the temptation in people to accept as truths their culture's fantasies. Warning his readers about the danger that lies in turning art into dogma, Coover writes:

> Castille is a fairytale tierra
> where peasants pray in cold castles
>   and kings live in crosses . . .
>   Maria makes magic fiestas;
>   in gold bracelets she passes and blesses
>   the laboring classes . . .
>   The sunwitch's trances (siestas)
>   are broken by potions from presses
>   in microbial glasses . . .
> But when fairtale folk become fiera
> none can calm the irascible vassals
> —nor all the king's horses . . .[9]

"Quenby and Ola, Swede and Carl" does not reinterpret a fairy tale, but the context in which Coover's fiction takes place is a familiar one. Swede and Quenby live with their teenage daughter, Ola, on the banks of an isolated lake. They earn their living by hosting hunting and fishing expeditions for which Swede acts as a guide. Carl, who comes to the lake every summer for a week or two of fishing, is from the city. Narrated in the same fragmented form as "The Gingerbread House," "Quenby and Ola, Swede and Carl" opens with an ominous description of a boat on a lake. The story's second fragment focuses the reader's attention on Quenby and Ola, who are working at a barbecue pit, but the narrator's directive, "Imagine" (PD, p. 150), makes the reader wonder whether the scene is a fantasy and, if so, whose. Fragment three introduces Carl, who is sitting in the bow of the boat on the lake, but the reader does not learn that Swede is with him until the seventh fragment. Between these two scenes are a description of an island on the lake, a sexual encounter between two as yet unknown participants, and a description of the foliage on the islands in the area. Fragment eight concerns Ola, who is not at the barbecue pit but telling a group of people a story about her cat. Coover's narrator does not tell his readers whether this scene is real or imaginary. Through twenty-nine more fragments, Coover creates a story, or rather several stories, that take place in several locales over an indeterminable period of time and are, in part, the fantasy of several imaginations.

One of the stories, which seems to take place in the present, focuses on Carl and Swede, who are sitting in a stalled boat on an isolated lake in the black of night. Swede, who does not talk much, is not worried; Carl is, but not about the stalled motor. Sometime before setting out in the boat with Swede, Carl made love with Quenby and later went skinny-dipping with Ola. He suspects that Swede may have seen him with Quenby through a shutter the excited lovers forgot to close. Swede may also have been the one who took Carl's underwear while the man from the city was swimming with Ola. There is no way for Carl to be sure what Swede knows, but he suspects that Swede has brought him to an isolated part of the lake to kill him. Carl tries to mask his fear by participating in some of the macho conventions of fishermen. He "punches" cans of beer, "pisses" from the side of the boat, and tries to make conversation with Swede. The events of Carl's time with Swede, Quenby, and Ola as well as his thoughts are told from a third-person point of view, but occasionally Coover's narrator slips into a second-person monologue that gives the reader an insight into Carl's mind and, in a way, establishes a dialogue with him. This dialogue, in effect, brings the reader closer to Carl. It helps him understand and sympathize with the protagonist's responses to the sex-starved Quenby and blossoming Ola and the terror he senses while sitting in the boat:

You know what's going on out here, don't you? You're not that stupid. You know why the motor's gone dead, way out here, miles from nowhere. You know the reason for the silence. For the wait. Dragging it out. Making you feel it. After all, there was the missing underwear. . . . But what could a man do? You remember the teasing buttocks as she dogpaddled away, the taste of her wet belly on the gunwales of the launch, the terrible splash when you fell. Awhile ago, you gave a tug on the stringer. . . . The stringer felt oddly weighted. You had a sudden vision of a long cold body at the end of it, hooked through a cheek, eyes glasedover, childish limbs adrift. What do you do with a vision like that? You forget it. You try to. (*PD*, p. 161)

To further inhibit the reader from making an arbitrary moral decision regarding Carl's behavior, the narrator has Ola tell a story that reveals something of Swede's character and a good reason for Carl to fear him:

"I asked Daddy why he shot my cat," she said. . . . It was a sad question, but her lips were smiling, her small white teeth glittering gaily. She'd just imitated her daddy lobbing the cat up in the air and blowing its head off. " 'Well, honey, I gave it a sporting chance,' " he said, " 'I threw it up in the air, and if it'd flown away, I wouldn't have shot it!' " She joined in the general laughter, skipping awkwardly, girlishly, back to the group. It was a good story. (*PD*, p. 165)

In light of such insensitivity to life, it is no wonder why Carl is so afraid of Swede or why Quenby craves affection.

How the story ends, Coover's narrator, as he does in "The Door" and "The Gingerbread House," allows his readers to decide for themselves. The whole tale may have been imagined by Carl; certainly parts of it are, but what is the real story? Coover never says because it is not a question that he believes needs to be answered. What is important is the readers' response to the author's focusing their attention on the role of the fiction maker and the possibilities of appreciation that are afforded by the dismantling of conventional approaches to literature.

Those parts of "Quenby and Ola, Swede and Carl" that the narrator has chosen to relate end peacefully. Nevertheless, all is not well. As in "The Gingerbread House," which concluded with the sound of the witch's black rags flapping beyond the heart-shaped door, so too does this story about a series of events that may have never occurred end with a sound that beneath the rustic peace of the island causes Ola to wonder about the noise her cat made after it plummeted to the earth. What lies within the fiction maker's imagination may not be always pretty or capable of confirming his readers' already held viewpoints of the world, but it does contain a comment on the human condition that Coover believes is more true to life and consequently more valid than any "realistic" description.

"Morris in Chains" is similar to "Quenby and Ola, Swede and Carl" in that it begins at its end, is fragmented by the use of more than one narrative voice, and concerns a conflict between rustic and urban sensibilities. The story opens with an announcement to the nation that, under the command of Dr. Peloris, M.D., Ph.D., U.D., agents of the state have captured Morris and shot his sheep. By announcing the outcome of the chase that the story details, Coover's narrator loses an element of suspense, but quickly gains the reader's sympathy for Morris as well as an appreciation of the tension that exists between the shepherd's pathetic solutions to his predicament and his eventual end. Heightening the tension and enriching the pathos are the two narrative voices Coover uses to relate the fragments of his story. The first voice, that of the scientific agents of the community, is third-person and objective: "There were early crises, these have been admitted. No one doubted the eventual outcome, of course: it was merest Morris versus the infallibility of our computers, after all. Data properly gathered and applied must sooner or later worst the wily old cock" (*PD*, p. 48). Morris's voice, on the other hand, is first-person, subjective, and informal. Its loose punctuation, stream-of-consciousness style, and idiosyncratic expressions reflect the shepherd's natural state: ". . . God knows *I* ain't got no mission! just alfalf and lotus that's all I'm seeking and these days it's damn hard to come by I can tell you . . ." (*PD*, p. 47).

Morris's music, unconventional life-style, imagination, and preoccupation with the nonscientific side of nature threaten the highly organized, technological position of the state. The citizenry is still susceptible to some of the old temptations. New flocks are forming; new pipes are heard. As a result, Dr. Peloris tries to capture Morris, who escapes from his hunters for short periods of time but suffers from the pressure they bring to bear upon him and his flock. At one point in his escape, Morris is forced to leave behind a ewe who is too old to keep up with the fleeing flock. On another occasion, Morris is forced to commit the unnatural act of castrating his ram, who was doing such a good job inpregnating the sheep that Morris could not effectively elude Dr. Peloris's agents. The pain Morris feels in committing the act that has been forced upon him by the insensitive community is accentuated by the shepherd's virile affection for women of all shapes and ages. His ultimate degradation, then, is not his capture, which he accepts quietly, but the community's clinical examination of his semen.

Like most of the stories in this collection, "Morris in Chains" is a simple tale, the importance of which lies not so much in its events as its innovative narrative techniques and rational comments on human nature and fiction. The fragmented episodes of this story reflect a stage of enriched development that "The Gingerbread House" and "Quenby and Ola, Swede and Carl" lacked. On the other hand, Coover's more complete fragments approach rather than distance themselves from traditional narrative forms. Similarly, his endorsement of "the sin of the simple" (*PD*, p. 49) seems to contradict the literary acrobatics of many of his previous works. Morris's fate is equally as confusing. Is investigation by the scientific community the humiliating end of writers who return to myths to forge new perspectives on society or is Coover satirizing his belief that myths should be abandoned when they are no longer useful? Perhaps the one consistent element that "Morris in Chains" shares with the rest of Coover's pricksongs and descants is its ambiguity. By associating Morris with the forest Little Red Riding Hood, Hansel and Gretel had to avoid to participate in the adult world, Coover, like Walt Whitman, may be saying, "You say I contradict myself? Very well I contradict myself."

"The Romance of the Thin Man and the Fat Lady" reexamines a traditional metaphor, and, like "Morris in Chains," makes a comment on the loss of identity that can be suffered whenever conventions rule:

Now, many stories have been told, songs sung, about the Thin Man and the Fat Lady. Not only is there something comic in the coupling, but the tall erect and bony stature of the Man and the cloven mass of roseate flesh that is the Lady are in themselves metaphors too apparent to be missed. To be sure of it, one need only try to imagine a Thin Lady paired with a Fat Man. It is not only ludicrous, it is unpleasant. No, the much recounted mating of the Thin Man with the Fat Lady is a circus legend full of truth. In fact, it is hardly more or less than the ultimate image of all our common everyday romances, which are also, let us confess, somehow comic. (*PD*, p. 138)

Not even "Ultimate Heroes" (*PD*, p. 142) such as these, however, are free from the dictates of fashion. The Thin Man wishes to develop muscles to excite the Fat Lady; she, in turn, wants to lose weight so she can be more appealing to her lover. Fashion notwithstanding, a muscular Thin Man and a slender Fat Lady spell financial ruin for the Ringmaster, a sort of Dr. Peloris of the circus world. Unfortunately for the Ringmaster, the circus community cannot blame the lovers for creating their own world, and, without the Thin Man's and Fat Lady's knowledge, murder their "Keeper of the Holier Books" (*PD*, p. 140). Unfortunately for the lovers, the audience that comes to see the freak show is not as egalitarian as the circus people. Dictators of the Ringmaster, they come to see the thinnest of men and the fattest of ladies and do not permit the lovers to alter their identities. In order to bring money into the circus, that is, survive, the Thin Man and the Fat Lady must consistently satisfy the expectations of their audience, which acts as a sort of mass custom agent working to prevent originality from entering the culture.

Depressed by the audience's veto of their freedom, the Thin Man cannot lose the muscles he built up and the Fat Lady cannot gain back the weight she lost. Suspecting each other of being narcissistic and disloyal to the circus community, they quarrel. Eventually the Fat Lady is sold to another circus. At this point in the story, the narrator, who sees that the important "metaphor . . . has come unhinged" (*PD*, p. 146), calls for a rescue. Providing for his readers and the lovers a *deus ex machina*, the narrator reunites the Thin Man and the Fat Lady. Their story, however, does not end happily. Like the Universal Baseball Association's creator, Henry, who also went to extreme lengths to maintain his metaphor, the narrator of "The Romance of the Thin Man and the Fat Lady" becomes irritated when he discovers the limits of his heroes. The "ludicrous," he says, "is not also beautiful" (*PD*, p. 147). Having lost the magic of their original metaphor, the Thin Man and the Fat Lady are relegated to another role, that of riding a rocket. Whereas the old metaphor fails to satisfy the audience, which has been enlightened by the ludicrous and now only pities or is repulsed by it, so too does any permutation. Eventually, the rocket upon which the Thin Man and the Fat Lady ride crashes and kills them both and perhaps the audience as well.

The central conflict in this story is, of course, between the lovers and the audience, but the confrontation is also a comment on the dogmatic power of arbitrary conventions. The Thin Man and the Fat Lady want to be conventionally beautiful and foolishly sacrifice their identities to meet a fashionable norm. Isolated from themselves, they become alienated from each other even as they try to satisfy the demands of people who insist on having their perspectives of life confirmed. By not allowing the lovers to explore the ranges of their identities, however, the people who support the circus imprison themselves in a limited viewpoint that eventually destroys any opportunities for change that may exist.

In addition to its attack on the limitations of fashion and its call for a return to a "taste for the simple" (PD, p. 147), "The Romance of the Thin Man and the Fat Lady" marks another step in Coover's development of narration through fragmented images. Interspersing the traditional narrative style of Coover's speaker are series upon series of comments made by unidentified members of the circus community. These comments serve to confirm what the narrator has just related to his reader. For example, when the narrator wants to reunite the Thin Man with the Fat Lady, he suggests that the man

is suddenly deposed, never mind why or how
    "Taking everything for himself."
    "Even started growing a moustache, bought himself a whip!"
    "We had a meeting and—"
Never mind. . . . The Man is exiled to the rival circus in exchange for a Family of Webfooted Midgets. (*PD*, p. 146)

When the couple is together again, the

image is made whole!
    "Beautiful in spite of all history!"
    See how their joyful tears flow!"
    "Oh! I'm all weepy and excited myself!" (*PD*, p. 146)

Ironically, the narrator's voice, which remains distinct from the circus people's and, in fact, often seems to dictate their responses, metamorphoses into that of the ringmaster's at the end of the story. As in so many of his stories, Coover concludes "The Romance of the Thin Man and the Fat Lady" on a note of terror that never seems to be far beneath the surface of human experience. Nevertheless, Coover's destruction of conventions is not without its rewards: " 'Suddenly it hits you see. All your life you been looking at circuses and you say that's how circuses are. But what if they ain't? What if it's all open-ended . . .' " (*PD*, p. 142).

Open-endedness is the primary concern of "The Magic Poker," a fiction told in fragments that mark Coover's departure from the reinterpretation of familiar stories and metaphors as his central focus to the infinite number of technical and imaginative alternatives available to writers who are able to create works that are free from conventional restraints. The story begins with Coover's most self-conscious narrator since "Klee Dead" establishing the limits of his control over the events that follow: "I wander the island, inventing it. I make a sun for it and trees . . . and cause the water to lap the pebbles of its abandoned shores . . . I impose a midday silence, a profound and heavy stillness. But anything can happen" (*PD*, p. 20). Eager to interest the reader in his story and teach him something about the creative process at the same time, the narrator frequently interrupts his story to emphasize its artificial quality: "Bedded deep in the grass, near the path up to the first cabin, lies a wrought-iron poker. It lies shadowed . . . by the grass that has grown up wildly around it. I put it there" (*PD*, p. 21). Although a self-proclaimed stickler for detail, Coover's narrator occasionally forgets some of the elements of his creation: "But where is the caretaker's son? I don't know. . . . This is awkward. Didn't I invent him along with the girls and the man in the turtleneck shirt" (*PD*, p. 27)? At times, the narrator allows his imagination to wander farther than he had intended and must bring it back under his control: "Wait a minute, this is getting out of hand! What happened to that poker, I was doing much better with the poker, I had something going there. . . . Back to the poker" (*PD*, pp. 29-30). On other occasions the narrator forgets that his story is a product of his imagination and confuses it with reality: "I begin to think of the island as somehow real. . . . I find myself peering into blue teakettles. . . . I wonder if others might come here without my knowing it. . . . Where does this illusion come from, the sensation of 'hardness' in a blue teakettle or in an iron poker . . ." (*PD*, pp. 33-34). Not surprisingly, Coover's readers also confuse reality with fiction: "Why this island sounds very much like the old Dahlberg place on Jackfish Island up in Rainy Lake, people say, and I wonder: can it be happening?" (*PD*, p. 40). Like J. Henry Waugh, the narrator of "The Magic Poker" watches as his fiction begins to take on a life of its own as well as a geographic locale. Gradually, however, the fiction reduces the importance of the narrator. Once the story is in control of itself, the number of directions in which it can go are limitless:

Once upon a time, a family of wealthy Minnesotans bought an island on Rainy Lake up on the Canadian border. . . .

Once upon a time there was an island visited by ruin and inhabited by strange woodland creatures. . . .

Once upon a time, two sisters visited a desolate island. . . .

Once upon a time there was a beautiful young princess in tight gold pants, so very tight in fact that no one could remove them from her. . . . (*PD*, pp. 40-42)

Providing additional comments on the role of the narrator and the attitude through which fiction should be approached are the characters of "The Magic Poker." Their story begins with two sisters who have come to visit the deserted mansion that exists on the island Coover has invented. Observing the sisters from various points on the island are the caretaker's son and a man wearing a turtleneck shirt. These four viewpoints of the events that occur become increasingly confusing to the reader as the narrator blurs realistic elements with imaginative ones. By creating a situation in which the reader cannot distinguish between what exists in the story and what takes place in its characters' minds, Coover seems to be saying that since fiction is a product of the imagination, anything that takes place within a story is possible and should be considered valid. For example, there are five versions of the girl with the gold tight pants finding the magic poker. The first time she comes across the poker, she kisses it and the man with the turtleneck shirt appears. The second time, she lifts it from the ground, is horrified by the number of insects that are living under it, and drops it. When the girl with the gold pants discovers the magic poker in the third version, she kisses its tip and again a man appears. In the fourth version, however, the girl kisses every part of the poker, but nothing happens.

Although only two of these versions seem plausible, they all contain narrative possibilities and must be considered as valid parts of the story. Uniting these alternatives with others, the poker, depending on the story read, may represent any one of an infinite number of possibilities, including a pen, a sword, a prince, a penis, and a magic wand. Furthermore, none of these possibilities is ever concluded. Each remains an open-ended challenge to the imaginations of Coover's readers.

Through his narrator's descriptions of the sisters, Coover presents an attitude through which his readers can increase their appreciation of fiction. The girl with the gold pants, loose blouse, silk scarf, and high heels has allowed the dictates of fashion to inhibit her movements on the island. She continually lags behind her more sensibly equipped sister, Karen. After three marriages, the fashion-minded sister is still a girl. Looking for princes rather than people she is, in the words of Neil Schmitz, "hysterically frigid, caught between desire and fear. Her idealized image of an urbane and fatherly protector blurs repeatedly into that of a brutish lover."[10] Interestingly, the girl's ambivalent attitude toward sex may very well reflect the tension between the narrator's desire to be creative and his fear of losing control of his material. In the case of "The Magic Poker," the narrator succumbs to the demands of his fiction and, in the process, emancipates himself from the literary traditions that the old mansion with its poorly tuned piano symbolizes. Apparently, Coover wishes that his readers would stop trying to make music out of obsolete instruments and, by stripping themselves of conventional approaches to literature, encounter his fictions prepared to have their imaginations challenged.

In "Beginnings," a fiction that is not included in *Pricksongs and Descants*, Coover challenges his readers to suspend their disbelief and accept a story about a writer who, "in order to get started" on a work he has in his mind, "went to live alone on an island and shot himself. His blood, unable to resist a final joke, splattered the cabin wall in a pattern that read: It is important to begin when everything is over."[11] In other words, once people kill the rigidifying conventions with which they approach literature, they will be able to enjoy fictions that have been enriched by infinite numbers of imaginative possibilities.

Beginning a story, says Coover's narrator, is always difficult because, traditionally, a beginning implies an end. By beginning his story with an end, however, and later ending it with a beginning, the narrator achieves a sort of constant middle in which virtually anything can happen: a man is born at the age of thirty-two with a self-destruct mechanism in his gonads; the writer begins a story in which the first-person narrator is the story itself; a friend of the writer borrows his typing ribbon for a clothesline and mistakes his story for a grocery list, nearly poisoning them both; Jesus cannot raise Lazarus from the dead and is embarrassed in front of a crowd of expectant onlookers; God turns Noah into salt; a soldier who has been in a foxhole for fifty years forgets who the enemy is, crawls out of his hole one day, and is shot; to keep Adam from starving, Eve turns herself into an apple. There are more stories, but Coover's point is made: whether the stories are plausible, concern what the protagonist does or what the characters do, they all contain narrative possibilities that, because they take place within the context of a fiction, are also valid. Moreover, Coover, as he did in "The Magic Poker," does not conclude any of the possibilities he presents. Each remains, as Coover believes fiction should be, an open-ended challenge to his readers' imaginations.

Compared with the complex mataphor of "The Magic Poker," "The Elevator" seems almost regressive after a first reading. Written before any of the other stories discussed in this chapter, "The Elevator," says Coover, "became the generative idea, and eventually led to several new fictions which brought the book together" (Gado, p. 151). This simplest of Coover's fragmented fictions introduces Martin, a dullard for whom the small compressed room in which he travels is an arena within which he experiences the most crucial events of his life. For Coover, the elevator is a universe of narrative possibilities.

Predictably, "The Elevator" is divided into fifteen fragments, one for each of the floors in Martin's building plus the basement. Combined, these fragments present several experiences in Martin's life that serve as a metaphor for his entire being. To try to distinguish which of these events is real and which is imagined is futile and inconsequential. All of the events are real because of their importance to Martin and the representation Coover gives them. They are not presented sequentially but are juxtaposed with one another to create the effect of each story having several versions. The result is a picture of the human condition as seen through a variety of forms: fantasy, romance, reality, daydream, and nightmare. Thus, "The Elevator" presents in its structure a central concern of all Coover's works, namely, the importance of variety as a means of combating man's tendency to reduce life and fiction to simple terms that he can understand but which inevitably fail him because of their limited perspective.

Over the course of the story, the reader learns that for seven years Martin has wanted to take the elevator to the basement instead of the fourteenth floor. Snorting at his timidity, he presses the "B" button one day and imagines he is descending into hell, but when the automatic doors open, he sees nothing. The basement is empty, silent, and meaningless. In the seventh fragment, Martin presses the number "1" button on the elevator's panel, but arrives at the fifteenth floor. Like the basement, the unknown region of Martin's being is utterly dark, but as shapes begin to form, the man panics. Afraid of anything that does not exist within the well-tread confines of his small world, Martin tells himself that there is no fifteenth floor.

Within the totality of Martin's universe, several events replay themselves. Frequently, the incurious office worker is the brunt of an ongoing joke perpetuated by a man named Carruther and his fellow workers. Impotently, Martin suffers their abuse until he thinks of a retort that earns him a knuckle sandwich and embarrasses him in front of a pretty elevator operator whose attention he has been seeking. Martin's only defense against this sort of humiliation seems to be the restorative powers of his limited imagination. The fourteenth fragment of the story, for example, records an improbable conversation in which Carruther is quoted as having tremendous respect for the size of Martin's penis. As might be expected, fantasies of this kind do wonders for the impotent worker's ego. In fact, Martin becomes so powerful he is able to allow his elevator's occupants to fall to their deaths: *"In the end,"* says Martin, *"doom touches all! MY doom! I impose it! TREMBLE!"* (*PD*, p. 134).

Coover, as has become his practice, concludes his story with a comment on the role of the fiction maker. Martin's destruction of his world in the final fragment of "The Elevator" establishes the fact that he has maintained enough power over his characters to eliminate them if they disappoint him, but by not freeing himself from the conventions of his art and allowing his personae to develop an existence that goes beyond their creator's control, his invented fiction fails to explore the nether region of human experience that lies beyond the familiar. Unlike Martin, Coover tends "to give in to the demands of the metaphor—or to the grouping of metaphors that, at times, seems to be creating the fiction for me . . ." (Gado, p. 158). In spite of the metaphor that Martin has destroyed, "The Elevator" maintains one of its own, namely, a structure that is capable of containing an infinite number of possibilities, and, apparently, Coover depends as much on his readers as himself to use whatever devices are available to explore the possibilities of fiction and reality that frighten Martin and keep him forever conventional and impotent.

The least complicated and most shallow of all Coover's narratives, "A Pedestrian Accident" comes astonishingly close to being a perfect example of the kind of narrative its author has been encouraging his readers to avoid. Originally published as "Incident in the Streets of the City," the story begins, uncharacteristically, at a beginning: "Paul stepped off the curb and got hit by a truck" (*PD*, p. 183). Trapped beneath the truck's wheels, Paul watches in disbelief as a policeman makes a fool of himself in front of a crowd that has gathered by seriously recording the nonsensical, self-inflating words of Charity Grundy. A gin-smelling egotist, who crossed "The Grand Climacteric" years ago, Mrs. Grundy uses Paul's unfortunate accident to entertain the crowd and establish herself as the center of its attention: " 'Officer,' she gasped. 'He was my lover!' . . . 'We met . . . just one year ago today. O fateful hour! . . . He was selling seachests, door to door. I can see him now as he was then, . . . chapfallen and misused, orphaned by the rapacious world, yet pure and undefiled . . . perspiration illuminating his manly brow, wounding his eyes, wrinkling his undershirt' " (*PD*, p. 191). Unfortunately for the reader, Paul and no doubt Coover, too, are fascinated with Mrs. Grundy and allow her to continue her story. Interspersing Grundy's monologue are crowd-pleasing confrontations between the old woman and the policeman as well as repetitive statements by the driver of the truck that hit Paul. One of these statements, "Boy I seen punchies in my sweet time but this cookie takes the cake God bless the laboring class I say and preserve us from the humble freak" (*PD*, p. 194), serves as a good example of just how weak Coover's satire on middle-class sensibilities is.

A doctor finally arrives at the scene of the accident, but he offers little relief to either Paul or the reader. As tiresome as Mrs. Grundy, the policeman, and the truck driver, the doctor performs a rudimentary examination of Paul, orders the truck to back up over the fallen pedestrian, and threatens everyone within the sound of his authoritative voice with the consequences of not obeying him. Of course, he does little good; even the priest he orders to appear fails to show up. Eventually, Paul passes out from the pain. When he awakens, the crowd has dispersed. Except for the truck that hit him, only a beggar and a dog are visible. The beggar waits for Paul to die so he can have his clothes; the dog, who is famished, cannot afford to be patient or considerate. Seeing that he has been struck by a truck from the Magic Lipstick Company, Paul ponders his ironic end and wonders how much longer he will suffer as the dog tears away and begins chewing a slice of flesh from the victim's cheek.

Speaking of his goal in writing pieces of this kind, Coover says, "If we are moved by nightmarish fiction, I mean when something hits us strong enough, it means it's something real. Otherwise we look at it and say it's a cute act, you know, but it doesn't touch me at all. But sometimes it hits inside—that means there's something there that is part of reality and the author is demonstrating that and that's where the contact is, communication across reality links, not across conventional links which is what most writing is made up of and what most second rate writers make, you know, things you'd expect, you know how the endings are going to be. But that's not what art, real art, reaches" (Hertzel, p. 27). That "A Pedestrian Accident" contains an unexpected ending, is not "cute," and presents a recognizable part of reality through the quality of its "nighmarish" plot cannot be denied. Nevertheless, it is a second-rate story. Its theme of humor brought about by extremity is presented more effectively in *The Universal Baseball Association, Inc., J. Henry Waugh, Prop.*, in which Coover created a tension between the novel's action and its participant's emotions that is absent here. The story's single, nontraditional narrative technique, that of using the voices of unidentified characters to comment on the events surrounding the accident, is developed more extensively in "The Romance of the Thin Man and the Fat Lady." Questionably intellectual, crude, and lacking sensitivity, "A Pedestrian Accident" might be labeled regressive if there was one less mature story in this collection of short fiction.

If "A Pedestrian Accident" is the weakest of Coover's pricksongs and descants, "The Babysitter" is by far his most successful. Narrated omnisciently in a voice that frequently assumes the speech patterns of the characters it describes, Coover's pricksong centers on a relatively common situation: a babysitter arrives, the parents leave for a party, and the babysitter begins bathing the children before putting them to bed. The descant that revolves around this central plot line involves a series of real and imagined events that manipulate for the reader's and author's pleasure a variety of contemporary society's stock neuroses.

That the fears and desires of Coover's characters are manifested through sex and violence should not be surprising. William Gass summarizes the fabulous plot of the story this way:

She arrives at seven-forty, but how will her evening be? ordinary? the Tucker children bathed and put away like dishes, a bit of TV, then a snooze? Or will she take a tub herself, as she seems to have done the last time? Will she, rattled, throttle the baby to silence its screaming, allow it to smother in sudsy water? and bring a sadistic friend? Or maybe a mysterious stranger will forcibly enter and enter her? No— she will seduce the children; no—they will seduce her; no—Mr. Tucker, with the ease and suddenness of a daydream, will return from the party and (a) surprise her in carnal conjunction with her boyfriend, (b) embrace her slippery body in the bath, (c) be discovered himself by (i) his wife, (ii) his friends, (iii) the police . . . or . . . All the while the TV has its own tale to tell, and eventually, perhaps, on the news, an account will be given of . . . While the baby chokes on its diaper pin? While the sitter, still warm out of water, is taken by Mr. Tucker? While both she and the children are murdered by Boyfriend and Friend? No. . . .[12]

Though Gass's cleverly detailed synopsis represents only a fraction of the story's events, his point is clear: "The Babysitter" includes anything anyone wants to imagine takes place in and around the Tucker's house from seven-forty to ten o'clock on this particular night. If what the reader is looking for has not occurred at the drugstore, in the pinball machine, on the television, outside the bathroom window, on the telephone, at the party the Tuckers are attending, or in the bathtub, he can probably find it in one of the characters' fantasies or in one of his own. In Gass's words, "our author says yes to everything."

In addition to presenting a mature composite of most of the techniques he introduced in his other fragmented stories, Coover includes in "The Babysitter" several combinations of these narrative styles. For example, in one fragment, Coover not only presents the real and imagined events of a character, he intermingles them with those of two other personae: " 'Stop it!' she screams. 'Please stop!' She's on her hands and knees and Jack is holding her down. 'Now we're gonna teach you how to be a nice girl,' Mark says and lifts her skirt. 'Well, I'll be damned!' 'What's the matter?' asks Jack, his heart pounding. 'Look at this big pair of men's underpants she's got on!' 'Those are my daddy's' says Jimmy, watching them from the doorway. 'I'm gonna tell' " (*PD*, p. 231). Seemingly simple, this brief exchange represents the tip of an iceburg that is being supported by the reader's assimilation of all that has led up to it. The first words spoken are the babysitter's, but they may exist in the mind of Jack, who imagines himself protecting his girlfriend from his would-be rapist partner, Mark. On the other hand, the babysitter's words may be imagined by Mark, for whom a struggle is part of the thrill of rape. Wearing Mr. Tucker's underwear, however, is a fantasy of the babysitter that Jack, her boyfriend and protector, has no knowledge of. Are the words, then, as they first seemed, the babysitter's? Do they take place in her imagination? Does she fantasize being raped by the two boys? Does she think Jack will protect her? Is it really Mr. Tucker she wants? Did he put her in his underpants? Is this his fantasy? Does Jimmy really see the babysitter wearing his father's underwear or is the teenager imagining how embarrassed she would be if the boy told his father what she had done? But did she put the father's underwear on in the first place? Was she not just looking at them when Jimmy came into the bathroom? In any other Coover story, each of these alternatives would be considered a narrative possibility; in "The Babysitter," they all occur.

As these events expand in the reader's consciousness like a series of chain-reacting fireworks, Coover marks their progression in the time zone in which the story takes place. Between seven-forty and eight o'clock, the babysitter arrives and feeds the children, the Tuckers leave for the party, Mark and Jack play pinball and talk about rape, the children begin wrestling with the babysitter, and lovers in formal attire dance on the television. Within the next hour, the children find excuses for not going to bed, Mr. Tucker imagines himself making love to the babysitter whom Mrs. Tucker does not know if she trusts with the children, Jack and Mark rape and do not rape the babysitter whom Jack defends against Mark, the babysitter refuses to let the boys come over to the house after telling them they can, Mr. Tucker plans his seduction of the sitter, the lean-jawed sheriff on television gets a boot in the face, the babysitter cannot get Jimmy to take a bath but she allows him to wash her back while she bathes, the boys call the babysitter on the phone and watch from the bathroom window as she gets in and out of the tub, Mr. Tucker imagines Jack making love to the girl, rapes her himself, sends the boy home without any of his clothes, catches the boys hiding in the bushes and raping the babysitter, and sings "I dream of Jeannie with the light brown pubic hair." A spy movie is on television, but the babysitter knows she should do her school-work. The final hour of the evening chronicles variations of everything that has happened since seven-forty. In addition, everyone at the party the Tuckers are attending try to stuff Mrs. Tucker back into her girdle, Jack and Mark drown the babysitter who drowns and suffocates the baby. By the time the police arrive at the Tuckers' home, everyone but Mrs. Tucker is dead. The news is reported on the television, but Mrs. Tucker is more interested in what's playing on the late-night movie. The next day, the babysitter and the boys hear about the tragic news that was reported and are shocked. By the story's end, Coover's readers have been introduced to more narrative permutations than they can possibly remember. What keeps "The Babysitter" and its structural achievements from being considered as little more than a collection of fascinating technical tricks, however, is its characters' lack of any but the most superficial of human thoughts and emotions, a consistent failing in most of Coover's short fictions, and the story's slight social message, which informs its readers in no subtle terms that lust, violence, boredom, and deceit play a significant part in the real and imagined events of contemporary man.

Like one of the television programs that the babysitter might watch in the Tuckers' home, "The Hat Act" presents a series of technically engaging but emotionally sterile feats of magic. An appropriate symbol for Coover's idea of the role of the fiction maker in literature, the magician manipulates his materials to shock his audience's predetermined expectations of him and what is possible within the realm of his art:

Magician attempts to remove hat, but it appears to be stuck. Twists and writhes in struggle with stuck hat. . . . Finally, magician requests two volunteers from the audience. Two large brawny men enter stage from audience, smiling awkwardly. . . . One large man grasps hat, the other clutches magician's legs. They pull cautiously. The hat does not come off. They pull harder. . . . Magician's neck stretches, snaps in two: POP! Large men tumble apart, rolling to opposite sides of stage, one with body, the other with hat containing magician's severed head. . . . *Screams of terror.* . . . Decapitated body stands. . . . *Shrieks and screams.* . . . Zipper in front of decapitated body opens, magician emerges. . . . *Wild applause, shouts cheers.* (*PD*, pp. 243–45)

Once the horizons of their expectations have been broadened, however, the audience refuses to applaud anything less than a feat that outdoes all that have preceded it. Unfortunately, there is a limit to the magician's imagination. Having placed his lovely assistant inside of his hat, the magician cannot get her out. To his and the audience's horror, the assistant dies. Two men tie up the magician and drag him away, while members of the audience weep, vomit, and shout accusations of murder. Eventually, one of the men returns and sets up a placard that reads: "THIS ACT IS CONCLUDED. THE MANAGEMENT REGRETS THERE WILL BE NO REFUND" (*PD*, p. 256).

Obviously, Coover is not one to solicit his readers' approbation, but his self-reflexive comment on the author, his work, and his audience's ability to respond to his art in "The Hat Act" seems somewhat impertinent when compared with the tone he adapts in dedicating this collection of short fictions to Miguel de Cervantes Saavedra:

You teach us, *Maestro*, by example, that great narratives remain meaningful through time as a language-medium between generations, as a weapon against the fringe-areas of our consciousness, and as a mythic reinforcement of our tenuous grip on reality. The novelist uses familiar mythic or historical forms to combat the content of those forms and to conduct the reader . . . to the real, away from mystification to clarification, away from magic to maturity, away from mystery to revelation. And it is above all to the need for new modes of perception and fictional forms able to encompass them that I, barber's basin on my head, address these stories. If they seem slight for such a burden as this prolix forward, please consider them, in turn, *don* Miguel, as a mere preface to all that here flowers. . . . (*PD*, pp. 78-79)

Like his magician, Coover can perform feats of wizardry with the materials given him, but he is not always equal to the task to which he addresses himself. His "hat act," like the magician's assistant, dies because it lacks depth. It has no human voices to project the significance of its author's failure. As they are presented in this collection, Coover's fictions amount to little more than fascinating but impersonal mental exercises that might very well inspire some readers to request a refund. There are a few exceptions to this rule but hardly enough to counteract the overall impression of the artificial constructs. In terms of its aesthetic goal, then, this final circus of manic possibilities serves as a metaphor of the author's primary concern in all of the pricksongs and descants. Emphasizing the technical possibilities available in fiction and the new perspectives of literature and life that they provide, Coover focuses most of his attention on what is magic rather than what is human in art. Like those of any brilliant magician, Coover's narrative tricks seem effortless. "Really there's nothing to it," says the narrator of "The Magic Poker." "In fact, it's a pleasure" (*PD*, p. 22).

CHAPTER 4

The Later Works

I   A Theological Position

"**L**UCKILY, I DON'T have to teach anybody, so I don't have to know anything. I'm not obliged to read for any extrinsic means. I've never had this kind of connection to literature—I never even took lit courses. So if I pick up a book called *The Iliad* and I'm bored by it, I just put it down. If I go on reading, it's because it's alive for me now.

"Fiction is alive to a fiction maker in a different way. What comes through is the dedication the guy had to his craft, the extent to which he was captivated by what he was working on, the honesty with which he faced his narrative problems, and so on. A book that is dull to others may be fascinating to a writer who can observe this other craftsman struggle and devise solutions. In contrast, some books that are quite celebrated may hit the novelist as boring because they don't engage his interest at the level of craft" (Gado, p. 146).

In light of the novels and short fictions that have preceded it, *A Theological Position* represents an extent to which Coover's dedication to his craft may be measured. As he has done since committing himself to narrative structures, Coover sallies forth to defend the fiction-making process against the dogmatic imperatives of convention. Accepting this role as an artist, he says, "gave me an excuse to be the anarchist I've always wanted to be. I discovered I could be an anarchist and be constructive at the same time" (Gado, p. 157). Challenging his reader's conventional vision of the world by creating parodies of stories with which he is familiar, Coover also dramatizes how necessary fictions are to the human imagination. More than aesthetically admirable, they are a kind of utility that man relies upon to enrich his life. When man loses sight of the fictional nature of his creations, however, he tends to dogmatize them. Consequently, the forms in which these fictions appear become rigid and resist the appearance of new constructs and the fresh ideas that usually accompany them. The point at which narrative forms become dogmatic, Coover is saying, also marks the time for them to be broken up and have their energies released into new perspectives. These new perspectives, however, represent more than a variety of views regarding narrative constructs; they are also metaphors through which life can be further comprehended and appreciated.

Coover's battle against conventional perspectives in the four one-act plays that are collected under the title *A Theological Position* follows a line of attack that is similar to the one he displayed in his campaign against the traditional narrative forms of the short story and the novel. Basically, Coover's attack is four-pronged: he begins by identifying the metaphor that has outlived its usefulness; he then demonstrates through parody the subjective nature of the metaphor and points out the danger of substituting fiction for truth; finally, he releases the imaginative forces that created the metaphor into new constructs. As Coover dismantles the popular culture's substitutions for truth, however, he paradoxically revitalizes them by providing new perspectives from which they may be approached. "Working with cultural givens and trying to improve upon them," he says, "is a rewarding endeavor. Sometimes a novel will coincide with the 'Head Start' cultural vocabulary of the broad audience; sometimes it won't. There's not much to be done about it, really. So I just have to continue the enterprise for itself. There will always be some people who will read such ventures, recognize value, and try to see that it is transmitted in one way or other" (Gado, p. 159).

In "The Kid," the first of what Coover calls "acts" to be presented in *A Theological Position,* the author demythifies Hollywood's version of the Wild West, but the short play does not mark its creator's first venture into life on the prairie. "The Duel," which originally appeared as "The Mex Would Arrive at Gentry's at 12:10," was first published in 1967.[1] Now more appropriately titled, the story opens with Sheriff Henry Harmon, a parody of the role Gary Cooper played in the film *High Noon,* fretting about the arrival in town of don Pedo, a Mexican antithesis of everything "Hank" stands for. To further emphasize the disparity that exists between his two protagonists, Coover gives each one his own narrative voice. Hank, as might be expected, is described in terms of the language and conventions the Mexican undercuts: "The sheriff of Gentry's Junction, erect, tall, lean, proud, his cold blue eyes squinting into the glare of the noon sun, walked silently, steadily alone, down the dusty Main Street, the jingle of his spurs muffled only slightly by the puffs of dust kicked up by his high heels." In contrast with Hank, don Pedo, whose name means "fart," is described by a voice that has been influenced by the Spanish language: "The wanted unwanted Mexican he stands at the bar. He laughs and laughs and he drinks. He is short to the extreme, nor is he lean. Squat. Squat is the word, and dark with brown watery eyes. Not severe. Not honest. . . . It is assumed that all the womans die beneath the Mexican, later or sooner. It is the, how you say? the legend."

While don Pedo throws into disarray the order and complete-ness of which the sheriff is so fond, Hank tries to round up a posse from among the townspeople, who seem to be more afraid of him than the fun-loving bandit. While the sheriff bullies the town's most prominent maintainers of the status quo, the banker, the storekeeper, and the minister, into covering him during his face-off with the bandit, don Pedo seems to be breaking up all of the town's conventional attitudes. He is seen burning the sheriff's legal papers, winning at cards with a hand of five aces, making love with Hank's virgin fiancée, and "demonstrating for the little school children the enormity and joyous function of his genital member" while their teacher is "bound and gagged to her desk. . . . They applaud in childish glee as the Mexican he with the prodigious protuberance destroys a something-or-other that the schoolmarm has been guarding for years: POP! there she goes."

In a showdown that in many ways resembles the final scene of Eugene Ionesco's *The Killer*, in which a detective captures a mass murderer only to be convinced by him that life is not worth living, the sheriff makes his stand against don Pedo. With every Western cliché having been accounted for, however, Coover reverses the conventional procedures that brought him to this point in the story. When Hank steps forth to challenge the bandit to draw on him, he notices that the villain is not standing spread-legged in the middle of the street, but sitting on a bucket, picking at his teeth, and playing with a watch. When Hank notices that the watch is his, the Mexican returns it to him without protest.

Reaching down to disarm don Pedo, Hank senses that everything seems wrong. The gunfight is not going according to the script. Villains are not supposed to fart while being arrested and their guns should have notches in their handles. The bandit's are old and rusty; one of them has no hammer. Tossing the guns away, Hank concludes that the Mexican is a fraud. When he signals his back-up crew to come forward and bring a rope to hang don Pedo, however, he hears a click. He reaches for his guns, but his holsters are empty. The Mexican has stolen the sheriff's pistols while being disarmed. Spinning toward the bandit, Hank's astonished face greets a silver bullet from his own gun. As the bandit rides off into the sunset, he can hear behind him the sounds of celebration. The storekeeper, the banker, and the preacher, those keepers of conventions and resisters of originality, "swing with soft felicity from scaffolds and the golden whiskey he runs like blood."

Three years after writing "The Duel," Coover offered his readers a more serious, more complex parody of the Hollywood cowboy in "The Kid." The central conflict of this act is between two archetypal characters: the tall, lean, conventional sheriff, much like Hank Harmon, and the mythological bandit-hero. To underscore the archetypal significance of these characters, Coover does not give them names, though The Kid is obviously an extension of the Western bandit, Billy the Kid. To further emphasize the stereotypical qualities of the play's central characters, Coover refers to each of the town's men as "cowpoke" and each of its women as "belle." The lines of these personae are indicated by number rather than by name. Predictably, the dialogue is as wonderfully cliché-ridden as the characters in the play, and Coover, as he did for Giovanni Bruno in *The Origin of the Brunists,* Long Lew in *The Universal Baseball Association, Inc., J. Henry Waugh, Prop.,* and the shepherd of "Morris in Chains," perpetuates the myth of The Kid through folksongs:

> Come hear the Kid's story,
> It's bloody and gory
> And it's shore tuh put hair on yore chest!
> He kin lick any man,
> And he don't give a damn!
> He's the Savior of the West!
>   He's the Savior of the West!

As might be expected, The Kid falls somewhat short of the
legend that precedes him. He is handsome and dresses well for
the part he plays, but he is also nervous, as controlled by the
power of his guns as it is by him, and, like the inarticulate
Giovanni Bruno, confused by the myth that is developing around
him. To the astonishment of the cowpokes and belles, The
Sheriff exposes the truth that lies behind the myth associated
with The Kid when he fatally wounds the befuddled youngster in
a duel. Having freed the townspeople from the illusion under
which they were living, The Sheriff expects the cowpokes and
belles to be grateful to him for having killed The Kid. Like Tiger
Miller, however, The Sheriff has underestimated the community's need for fiction and the control it has over them. Before
The Kid's body is cold, the citizens begin to mythify The Sheriff,
who tries to explain to them the danger of fictionalizing events.
Of course, the townspeople, like the Brunists who refused to see
the truth of Tiger Miller's newspaper article about them, do not
listen to the words of The Sheriff, hang him, and continue to
mythify his actions through the established legend of The Kid.
Ironically, the lawman, like the newspaper editor, is the savior of
a fictitious belief he sought to undermine. Similarly, Coover's
play comments on the popular culture's tendency to award
heroic status to characters whose life-affirming actions have all
the qualities of a "B" movie.

While "The Kid" mocks one of the popular culture's most
important clichés, "Love Scene" demonstrates the deadening
effect conventions can have on artists, their subject matter, and
their audience. The play concerns a director whose attempts to
energize his lifeless actors in a love scene are frustrated by the
couple's inability to respond to romantic clichés. After failing
several times to find the convention through which his actors can
free themselves from what he suspects are their inhibitions, the
director tries unsuccessfully to motivate them through romantic
allusions to history. Limited by his conventional perception of
love's emotion, however, the director cannot understand his
actors' inability to be moved by expressions and allusions that
have lost their potency. Recognizing the fact that his clichés
extinguish rather than spark the possibilities of love, the director
bitterly laments: "They're all used up. They're not worth shit
anymore" (*TP*, p. 97). Almost as if he were a fiction maker in the
process of a creation, the director provides a *deus ex machina* for

himself by ordering a technician to remove from the stage the couple that could not match his expectations. Like the narrators of "The Romance of the Thin Man and the Fat Lady" and "The Elevator," the director refuses to give in to the demands of his metaphor. As a result, he remains imprisoned in a world of language and fictional forms that are no longer capable of inspiring spontaneous expressions of emotion.

"Rip Awake," like "Love Scene," is a dramatic monologue that comments on the dangers of substituting fiction for truth. Like the director whose fictions cannot motivate his actors to feel, Coover's Rip Van Winkle is alienated from reality by the dreams he has come to believe in over the course of his long sleep. He believes he has conversations with people whom he later discovers to have been dead for years. People whom he knows to be dead, on the other hand, he resurrects within the context of his everyday reality:

And I'd wake up, alongside the river, a fishing pole in my hands instead of the beermug, and Dame Van Winkle pulling my ear and hollering at me to get back to my chores. Well now, I knew *she* was dead, . . . I knew it couldn't be her pulling on my ear like that, so I socked her on the head with my fishing pole and threw her in the river—get out of my wretched life, woman, once and for all! I hollered, Lord, I'd been wanting to do that for years, I felt as joyful as I'd felt since ever I dipped into that wicked flagon! Whoopee! And then, as she drifted away there, just under the water, I saw it wasn't that evil old wife of mine, after all, no, it was my daughter Judith, my own little girl, my dear little girl, oh my God, what has become of me . . . ? (*TP*, pp. 111–12)

Rip admits that his fantasies have their "sweet side," but his inability to prevent reality from intruding on what he has substituted for truth frightens him. Realizing that "there ain't *no* relief from having to watch things turning into themselves" (*TP*, p. 116), the old Dutchman tries to free himself from the fictions which he has come to believe. Eventually, Rip suspects his own fictional nature, but because he is unaware of Washington Irving's existence, he blames the gnomes for putting him to sleep and implanting in his mind the fantasies that have caused him so much trouble in what now he seems to consider his fictional reality.

As he has done in many of his short fictions, Coover has retold a familiar story from a new perspective. "Rip Awake," however, is also much like the final chapter of *The Unviersal Baseball Association, Inc., J. Henry Waugh, Prop.*, in which the ballplayers assume an existence of their own that goes beyond the control of their creation. Similarly, the Rip Van Winkle of Coover's story lives a life of alienation that exists beyond the pages of Washington Irving's story. Unlike Henry's baseball players, however, Rip is aware of his fictional nature. Believing that he is a product of the gnomes' collective imagination, he climbs their mountain in the hope that they will free him from his fictional characterization and allow him to be the person he thinks he is. In an article entitled "A Prisoner of Words," Neil Schmitz suggests that Coover may have intended "Rip Awake" to be a failed act, "to sound precisely the fatigue of his existential Van Winkle shouldering the absurd . . ."[3] To "sound precisely" the Sisyphean dilemna of modern existential man, however, can hardly be said to have failed. In fact, it is Rip's voice that makes his failure to resolve his situation so humanly significant, a quality that is severely lacking in many of the short stories collected in *Pricksongs and Descants.* Speaking of his dog, Wolf, his inability to distinguish between reality and fantasy, and the character the gnomes created that alienates him from himself, Rip says,

I do wish I had old Wolf along for company. . . . Old faithful Wolf. Well, I shot him. That's right. I didn't mean to, no, it damn near broke my heart, it was them little Dutchmen's fault again. . . . We were out hunting, I saw this beautiful stag. . . . Well you can guess easy enough how that one turned out. But by then, I'd got so used to things turning into other things, I just went on supposing Wolf *was* a stag, and I took him home and ate him, kept waiting for old Wolf to turn up again at the door. But he never did. He never did. (*TP*, pp. 103–12)

"A Theological Position," the work from which this collection receives its title, also concerns alienation and metamorphosis. The play opens toward the end of an argument in which a priest has stated the church's position against the possibility of a second virgin birth. Nevertheless, the wife of the man to whom the priest has been speaking is six months pregnant, and, though she has coupled with her husband, he has never experienced an ejaculation while inside her. Because the man's claims are antithetical to a belief the church accepts as true, the priest rejects them. (*TP*, p. 128). Even if the woman were an impregnated virgin, says the priest, sounding much like J, whose wife experienced an immaculate conception in "J's Marriage," or one of the ballplayers in the Universal Baseball Association, Inc., after Henry interfered with the league's natural course of events, the church "would not permit it! Not only would it be an intolerable interference in human existence, *intolerable,* I tell you, it would be heretical! . . . An act of perversion and historical depravity" (*TP*, p. 130). Having relayed to the couple the "spirit" of the church's law, the seemingly well-intentioned priest comments on its literal ambiguity and suggests that he have intercourse with the woman and relinquish her claim to virginity. That this coupling will take place six months after the woman's conception, says the priest, is an irrelevant technicality. The man agrees to let the priest make love with his wife, who, smiling demurely throughout most of the play, also consents. As the man and woman have anticipated, however, the priest can penetrate the pregnant virgin but he cannot ejaculate. Having been pulled by the man from the woman in whose vagina his penis had become stuck, the priest listens as the man explains that his wife's cunt has been talking for four months about how insensitive men are to women's needs, how their overly rational outlook prevents them from understanding experiences in life that lie beyond the realm of reason. "You've got about as much chance of fucking the world alive with that theological position of yours," says the cunt to the priest, "as you have of lighting a fire with mud" (*TP*, p. 163). The priest tries to quiet the cunt by placing his hand between the woman's legs, but the talking vagina bites him. When the priest threatens to burn the woman for witchcraft, the cunt says,

That's right, anything you don't understand, kill it, that's your road to salvation, your covenant with holy inertia! Kill and codify! (p. 169).

The priest and the man, who are no longer antagonists but allies against the woman who lets her cunt do her talking, do not want to recognize their emotional sterility. Refusing to accept his inability to ejaculate as a sign of his unwillingness to give of himself to another person, the priest, "IN GOD'S NAME" (*TP*, p. 171), plunges a knife into the woman's womb. For the first time in the play, she speaks through her mouth: "You . . . you have hurt me . . ." (*TP*, p. 171). This solution to the men's inability to understand, appreciate, and experience human emotion, says the cunt, has about as much a chance of success as trying to sign "your name by pissing into a sandstorm . . .!" (*TP*, p. 171). When the woman dies, the priest says a prayer for her soul, but before he and the man can leave the room, their pricks begin talking. "After all," says the voice from within the priest's robes, "there's something to be said for talking cunts . . ." (*TP*, p. 172).

The quality of reasonableness, which, according to Coover, can alienate man from life's emotional experiences, is central to "A Theological Position." Ironically presented through characters who have rationally accepted fiction as truth, the man and the priest, whenever they manage to overcome or suppress their anxiety, try to be reasonable in their conversation about the woman. "Oh," says the priest early in the play, "we are not trying to conjure away the misfortunate origins of all our sons, no, that is not what our mysteries portend, we wish only to liberate them from their primitive—and if I may be so blunt—their fetal attachments. . . . *It stands to reason!"* (*TP*, p. 129). The woman, on the other hand, has nothing to say to the reasonable men because her situation reflects a desire that cannot necessarily be formulated in words. To want to have a baby is a sensation that can be approached but not fully comprehended by reason. Nevertheless, the woman's position in the play is almost as ironic as the men's. She is not so rational as to substitute fiction for truth, but to want to bear a child in a world that is run by people who, in the name of god, exterminate whatever they do not understand *is* unreasonable.

Like Happy Bottom in *the Origin of the Brunists*, the talking cunt of "A Theological Position" points out the emotional sterility that exists in those who have become alienated from the genuinely human experiences in life; like the narrators of *The Universal Baseball Association, Inc., J. Henry Waugh, Prop.* and many of the stories in *Pricksongs and Descants*, the woman's "other mouth" warns against man's tendency to turn his fictions into dogmas. The plays collected in *A Theological Position* represent more than a summation of their author's themes to date, however. As in all of Coover's works, they focus the reader's attention primarily on the constructs in which they are placed. Rebelling against dramatic conventions with many of the same ideas he used to dismantle the traditional structures he found in novels and short stories, Coover ironically creates a narrative system of his own. Unlike conventional systems, however, Coover's designs are not closed entities. Though they unify the comments Coover makes on the human condition throughout his stories, novels, and plays, they also allow for an infinite variety of thematic and structural possibilities. No matter what the genre, Coover, like William Blake, seems to be saying, "I must create a system or be enslaved by another man's."

II The Public Burning

Having recast a variety of his favorite themes into the four plays collected in *A Theological Position,* Coover returned to *The Public Burning,* a novel he had been working on and publishing chapters from since the release of *The Origin of the Brunists* in 1966. "Having shaken off the most persistent of the stories that bothered me, I realized that other material which we take in as stories—newspaper articles, grade school histories, the things parents tell to teach us how to be good, TV programs, even societal notions that stamp some movement as good or bad—all had to be confronted in the same way. In fact, . . . *The Public Burning* . . . is a simple outgrowth of that Jesus thing I did at the beginning.

"I began it as a play, but then I thought it was awkward in that form; so, while I was finishing up the baseball book, I played with the idea as fiction. I put it off for a while because there was another book I wished to do first. Later, I wanted 'The Cat in the Hat for President, written in 1968, to come out as part of a book in election year 1972, and I needed a couple of novella-length things to go with it. I interrupted what I was doing and went back to the Rosenburg idea with that in mind, but then it expanded into something far too large for such a format.

"It is the story of June 19, 1953. On that day, the Rosenbergs are burned in Times Square and all the members of the tribe are drawn to the scene. All that has happened that day happens there, in a way; everything is condensed into one big circus event.

"Originally, it was the circus aspect that interested me most. Then I developed the idea of having the Vice President at the time become the first person narrator. The world has its superheroes—figures like Uncle Sam and the Phantom—and Richard Nixon, who wishes to be the incarnation of Uncle Sam but hasn't yet learned how to shazam himself into super-freakhood, is studying what is going on very carefully, picking up notes" (Gado, pp. 154–55).

As might be expected, a rendering of the Rosenbergs' electrocutions as the main attraction of a circus that features Richard Milhous Nixon as its principal clown became something of a publishers' hot potato. For more than a year after Coover had completed the manuscript, it was returned to him by publishers that had accepted the advice of their lawyers. Eventually, Richard Seaver and The Viking Press published the book in 1977.

Because neither Nixon nor the Rosenbergs' sons brought suit against Coover or his publishers, *The Public Burning* has been able to enjoy the success it merits on its own. Unlike Coover's earlier novels, which received mixed reviews from their first critics, *The Public Burning* was greeted by notices so similar to one another they seem as if they might have been written by one person. In his review for *Time* magazine, Paul Grey said, "Coover has won a campus reputation as an avant-gardist who can do with reality what a magician does with a pack of cards: shuffle the familiar into unexpected patterns." After having accused Coover of overwriting *The Public Burning,* Grey identified its author's major weakness as his inability to "touch hearts or minds instead of nerves. What might have been a long, compassionate book becomes a protracted sneer.[4] Larry McMurtry admired Coover's

brilliance in plenty, but this brilliance is like celestial lightning: it lights the sky but never really touches the earth where we live. . . . Why potentially great realists ignore the common chords that they can strike so resonantly in favor of the thin, repetitious strings of irony, satire, fable, and allegory is a very hard thing to figure out. That, however, is what Coover has done, and the result is one more ambitious bore.[5]

In an article entitled, "Coover's Revisionist Fantasy," Pearl K. Bell claimed that Coover's "inventive ferocity is aimed at the entire aggressively corrupt society. But the unrelenting malice . . . is tedious, not satirically destructive."[6] Thomas R. Edwards concluded his discussion of Coover's novel by saying, "This book is an extraordinary act of moral passion, a destructive device that will not easily be defused." Nevertheless, he tempered his praise by calling Coover's novel "a wasteful expenditure of creative energy. As a work of literary art, *The Public Burning* suffers from excess; it is considerably too long and repetitive. . . ."[7]

The prologue to Coover's most ambitious work since *The Origin of the Brunists* offers several good examples of Coover's brilliance turned into tedium. Speaking about the preparations being made for the auto-da-fé of the Rosenbergs, Coover's narrator creates a composite of the people, places, and things that reflects the American sensibilities of June 1953:

> An Entertainment Committee is appointed, chairmanned by Cecil B. De Mille, whose latest success was last year's Oscar-winning *Greatest Show on Earth*, with assistance from Sol Hurok, Dan Topping, Bernard Baruch, the AEC and Betty Crocker, Conrad Hilton, whose Alburquerque hotel figured prominently in the prosecution's case against the Rosenbergs, Sam Goldwyn and Walt Disney, Ed Sullivan, the director of the Mormon Tabernacle Choir, the various chiefs of staff, Sing Sing Warden Wilfred Denno, the Holy Six, and many more. They audition vocalists, disk jockeys, preachers, and stand-up comics, view rushes of Uncle Sam's documentary on the two little Rosenberg boys intended as a back projection for the burnings, commission Oliver Allstorm and His Pentagon Patriots to compose a special pageant theme song, assign a task force of experienced sachems to work up a few spontaneous demonstrations, and hire a Texas high-school marching band to play "One Fine Day" from *Madame Butterfly*, "The Anniversary Waltz," and the theme from *High Noon*, said to be a particular favorite these days of President Eisenhower (*PB*, p. 5).

Although Coover's hyperbolic vision of America in the early years of the Eisenhower administration can be astonishingly inclusive, his obsessive concern for and bombardment of his readers with the data he has culled from back issues of *Time* magazine, the *New York Times*, and the like often degenerates into an excessive recitation of names and events. Interspersing these pseudodocumented catalogues are the exhortations of Uncle Sam, a tiresome and unrelenting composite of patriotic chauvinism.

I am Sam Slick the Yankee Peddler—I can ride on a flash of lightnin', catch a thunderbolt in my fist, swaller niggers whole, raw or cooked,

slip without a scratch down a honey locust, whup my weight in wildcats
and redcoats, squeeze blood out of a turnip and cold cash out of a
parson, and out-inscrutabullize the heathen Chinee (*PB*, p. 6)

I cite this passage and the one that precedes it to present the
flavor of the two styles that Coover employs through half of his
novel's 534 pages and provide the reader with an example of the
tedious cataloging that has weakened the resistance of many
readers to hurry through these sections of *The Public Burning*
and enjoy the more personal and reflective chapters narrated by
Richard Nixon:

I believe in keeping my own counsel. It's something like wearing
clothing—if you let your hair down you feel too naked. Yet I longed for
this nakedness. My testing ground was Ola, the only steady girlfriend I
had before Pat. She was pretty, lively, exciting, she brought out my
more reckless side, in fact I loved her, but she couldn't get off the
merry-go-round, and I couldn't get on it. (*PB*, p. 298)

Dividing into four parts the twenty-eight chapters narrated by
Nixon and the ringmaster of Coover's circus are three "intermezzo" pieces that further contribute to the book's tiresome
display of technical wizardry. Rather than heightening the
horror and pathos of the Rosenbergs' situation, the artificial
quality of each intermezzo blunts the reader's emotional
response and focuses his attention on the construct within which
Coover presents the convicted spies condition. Coover's first
intermezzo renders into free-verse poetry a speech made by
President Eisenhower; his second presents a dramatic dialogue
in which Ethel Rosenberg and Eisenhower try to communicate
with each other by bouncing echoes of their public voices off the
audience they are addressing; the third intermezzo is "A Last-
Act Sing Sing Opera by Julius and Ethel Rosenberg," which
culminates in United States Marshals notifying the prisoners that
their executions have been set for the evening of their
fourteenth wedding anniversary.

Although the intermezzo segments are designed to make the
reader aware of what may have been occurring in the participants' consciousnesses on the days preceding the Rosenbergs'
execution, they more often than not repeat sentiments that have
been expressed in the novel's chapters. Consequently they
deaden the reader's visceral response to Coover's subject matter.

For example, Ethel Rosenberg, "rising to full power" in the novel's second intermezzo, exclaims, "Our sentences violate truth and the instincts of civilized humanity. The compassion of men sees us as victims caught in the terrible interplay of clashing ideologies and feverish international enmities" (*PB*, p. 251). The force with which this statement hits the reader, however, has been weakened by the number of similar statements that have preceded it. Earlier in the novel Julius Rosenberg states, "The world has come to recognize the true nature of our case and the people . . . are demonstrating . . . for peace and freedom" (*PB*, p. 101). Ethel, in a tone similar to the one with which she addresses President Eisenhower, writes: ". . . This is political prosecution, shameless, blatant, cynical. The executive arm of our government has become a party to murder" (*PB*, p. 101). *"Never let them change the truth of our innocence,"* write Julius to his lawyer, Manny Bloch. Jean-Paul Sartre calls the Rosenbergs victims of "legal lynchings" (*PB*, p. 103). His sentiments are echoed by Harold Urey, Albert Einstein, Justice William O. Douglas, Arthur Miller, students in Grenoble, professors at Oxford, movie directors from Rome, actors in London, peasants in Italy, and more. What people all over the world suspect when weighing the evidence against the Rosenbergs, Uncle Sam confirms: "Rig a prosecution? . . . Hell, *all* courtroom testimony about the past is ipso facto and teetotaciously a baldface lie, ain't that so? Moonshine! Chicanery! The ole gum game! Like history itself—all more or less bunk . . . ! Practical politics consists in ignorin' facts" (*PB*, p. 86). Even Vice President Nixon comes to recognize the Wagnerian scope of the Rosenbergs' trial:

. . . This was clearly a struggle between the forces of good and evil. . . . But there was more to it than that. Not only was everybody in the case from the Judge on down—indeed, just about everyone in the nation, in and out of government, myself included—behaving like actors caught up in a play, but we all seemed moreover to be aware of just what we are doing and at the same time of our inability, committed as we were to some higher purpose, some larger script as it were, to do otherwise. (*PB*, p. 117)

Though Ethel's appeal to President Eisenhower confirms Nixon's insight, her statement has been weakened by the numerous analyses that have led up to it. Rather than drawing the reader closer to the Rosenbergs' predicament, Coover's technically clever intermezzo desensitizes him through its simplistic repetition of what has been said better elsewhere in the novel.

Incorporating the boulders that lie in the reader's path with the more carefully paved road of the book is the premise upon which *The Public Burning* rests. Uncle Sam and the Phantom, a pseudonym for communism or anything else that challenges conventional thinking, are locked in a cold war that will establish the one or the other's supremacy in the world. In the middle of the 1940s, Uncle Sam was ahead of the Phantom by 443,000,000 people. By the end of the decade, however, the Phantom had pulled ahead of Uncle Sam. In spite of the Truman Doctrine, the Marshal Plan, and NATO, the Phantom exiled Chiang Kai-shek to Formosa, created America's first postwar recession, inspired the United States Secretary of Defense to kill himself, and exploded his first atomic bomb. Almost immediately, 600,000,000 people declared themselves neutral. In an attempt to explain how the Phantom was able to develop an atomic bomb before Uncle Sam had achieved control of the world, FBI director J. Edgar Hoover created the fiction of a Communist spy ring. With the help of Joseph McCarthy, Richard Nixon, Billy Graham, and the like, Hoover put America on the alert for the enemy within. Soon afterwards, the spy ring was broken and Julius and Ethel Rosenberg were arrested, tried, convicted, and sentenced to die for conspiring to give American military secrets to the Communists. The book opens with Uncle Sam rallying his followers around the two scapegoats for America's recent setbacks in the world and preparing to exorcise the Rosenbergs as spectacularly as possible. The electrocutions, a symbol of the extent to which Uncle Sam's light will battle the Phantom's darkness, are scheduled to take place in Times Square on the night of the Rosenbergs' fourteenth wedding anniversary. Various do-gooders try to gain clemency for the convicted spies, but their efforts, naturally, are blocked by the mainstream defenders of the American way of life. Uncle Sam's technologically impressive auto-da-fé becomes an orgy of mass hysteria, the central focus of which, ironically, is not the spies but Vice President Nixon, who, having just experienced a failed sexual encounter with Ethel Rosenberg, appears on the Times Square stage with his trousers around his ankles.

Sustaining most of the reader's interest through Coover's

broadly based plot and his chaotic pastiche of the topical junk gathered from newspapers, magazines, films, television and radio shows, Broadway plays, advertisements, popular songs, baseball scores, and the like are the novel's central characters: Richard Nixon, Uncle Sam, and the Rosenbergs. Of these the most successfully developed is the then Vice President, Coover's once and future link between Korea and Vietnam, between the 1950s and the 1970s: "My interest in Nixon—or my story about him— grew out of my concept of the book as a sequence of circus acts, bringing the show back down to the ground. You have a thrilling highwire number, and then the clown comes on, shoots off a cannon, takes a pratfall, drops his pants and exits. And then you can throw another high-wire act at them. So naturally I looked for the clownish aspects of my narrator, and you can't have an unsympathetic clown" (Wolff, p. 54). With an almost Chaplin-esque resourcefulness for recovery, Nixon struggles to maintain his dignity as he stumbles through the paces Coover has set for him. A genius for low comedy, Nixon acts like a dog for the amusement of his family, reveals his political naiveté on the golf course with Uncle Sam, who later interrupts the Vice President in the middle of a masturbatory fantasy, unwittingly smears himself with excrement, suffers the ad hominem jokes of a cab driver and Washington's press corps, unknowingly hands Uncle Sam an exploding cigar, discovers on a stage in Times Square that Ethel Rosenberg has written "I am a scamp" on his bare ass, and allows himself to be sodomized by Uncle Sam in order to be incarnated as President fifteen years after the events of the novel. Nevertheless, Nixon is more than just an agent through which Coover's readers can release the tension that has accumulated after watching events in a center ring. Though he maintains all of the qualities that make him so unloved by the public, he also elicits more sympathy than any of the novel's other characters and, as a result, steals the show. Speaking of the first year of his marriage to Pat, Nixon says,

Hitler was attacking Russia by the time we celebrated our first anniversary, and all I can remember from that time is the little apartment we had over a garage in Whittier, going to San Juan Capistrano and Santa Monica Beach . . . getting out of bed in the morning with Pat, sharing the bathroom, . . . mostly just exploring this new condition which I somehow thought of as unique in the world. (*PB*, p. 54)

Though the reader may cringe at statements such as, "I'm a lot like Lincoln, I guess, who was kind and compassionate on the one hand, and strong and competitive on the other," he cannot deny their human, at times pathetic, quality. An ineffable blend of want, need, fear, determination, hate, and sympathy, Nixon's self-revelations may well be Coover's major fictional achievement.

More of a cartoon figure than a character, Uncle Sam rants against communism or whatever else opposes his will for most of *The Public Burning*'s less successful chapters. A composite of phony affability, insensitivity, and opportunism, he tirelessly brays the metaphors of every Fourth-of-July orator:

So carry the flag, you sons a Liberty, hang on to yer balls and keep step to the music of the Union. . . . let us . . . show the world that a Freeman, contendin' for Liberty on his own ground, can out-run, out-dance, out-jump, chaw more tobacky and spit less, out-drink, out-holler, out-finagle, and out-lick any yaller, brown, red, black, or white thing in the shape of human that's ever set his onfortunate kickers on Yankee soil. (*PB*, pp. 7–8)

As much as Uncle Sam reveals about American lore, however, his rural idiom and singular perspective quickly cease to be amusing. Not until the novel's epilogue, when he admits his campaign against the Phantom is a hoax, does Uncle Sam awaken the reader's interest in him. Though only a caricature, he reveals himself to be an all-inclusive embodiment of a real evil in America, namely, the power and ability to interpret events for his own selfish purposes.

Unfortunately, the book's least successful characters, Julius and Ethel Rosenberg, could have been its most important. With the exception of the scene in which Ethel couples with Nixon, the convicts' experience of the trial and the days preceding their executions is engendered more from public records than Coover's imagination. Though often moving, their words lack introspection and occasionally seem rhetorical when compared with Nixon's pseudo-reflection. Alluding to the Nazi war criminals in her appeal for clemency, Ethel says, "Today, while these ghastly mass butchers, these obscene racists, are graciously receiving the benefits of mercy and in many instances being reinstated in public office, the great democratic United States is proposing the savage destruction of a small unoffending Jewish family, whose guilt is seriously doubted throughout the length and breadth of the civilized world" (*PB*, p. 251).

Of course, there is considerably less speech-making in the love letters the Rosenbergs exchange, but, as passionate as they are, the reader does not know the people who wrote them. They remain enigmas, almost, at times, artifacts. Unfortunately, what emotional force they generate comes more from the already held sympathies of the reader than anything that they say or do in the novel. Had he developed the Rosenbergs to an extent that approaches his characterization of Nixon, Coover might have touched more deeply his reader's willingness to sympathize with the victims' plight. As it is, Coover has relied on the Rosenbergs' electrocutions and the hoopla with which he surrounds them to shock the reader into compassion. Because he places his victims' deaths within a fabulously depicted scene designed to out-grotesque any that have preceded it, however, Coover's description of the executions is more disturbing when read outside of the novel's context: "Ethel Rosenberg's body, held only at head, groin, and one leg, is whipped like a sail in a high wind, flapping out at the people like one of those trick images in a 3-D movie. . . . Her body, sizzling and popping like fire-crackers, lights up with the force of the current, casting a flickering radiance on all those around her, and so she burns—and burns—and burns—as though held aloft by her own incandescent will and haloed about by all the gleaming great of the nation—" (*PB*, p. 517).

Although Coover's depiction of Nixon, Uncle Sam, the Rosenbergs, and the popular culture of America in the early 1950s seems to indicate a new direction in his work, *The Public Burning* is similar in plot, character, and theme to many of his earlier fictions. Though the ground covered in this most recent novel differs from that of Coover's other books, it is not unfamiliar to most readers. In addition, *The Public Burning*, like all of Coover's fictions, exposes the rigidity of literary conventions by focusing the reader's attention on Coover's idea of the fiction-making process, an open-ended system of infinite narrative possibilities. Unlike *A Theological Position*, which merely recasts many of Coover's familiar themes, however, *The Public Burning* does represent some development of the issues that have been of primary concern to Coover since he published *The Origin of the Brunists*.

Although less realistically portrayed in *The Public Burning*, the orgy that takes place in and around the pile of elephant dung in Times Square closely parrallels the mud-laden scene that occurs in *The Origin of the Brunists,* when the cult's members assemble on the Mount of Redemption to await the Final Judgment. In both cases, an archetypal victim of exploitation is killed and the novels' central figures are metaphorically castrated while the masses of people that are assembled celebrate in orgiastic fashion a ritual that has given their worlds a sense of order, meaning, and community. Similarly, Coover's second novel, *The Universal Baseball Association, Inc., J. Henry Waugh, Prop.,* ends with a ritual marking the passage of two deaths that have given the ballplayers in the league and their creator a sense of purpose. Here, too, there are suggestions of an orgy as female fans pull at the ballplayers' pants and succeed in separating a pair of them from its owner. In *The Origin of the Brunists,* West Condon miner Vince Bonali is caught not only with his pants down but in bed with a lonely woman whose husband has died in a recent mine disaster. Although the sexual exploitation of Wanda Cravens goes unmitigated, that of Ethel Rosenberg in *The Public Burning* does not as she manages to write "I am a scamp" on her exploiter's bare ass and expose his self-serving intentions to the crowd that has gathered in Times Square to watch her and her husband's electrocutions. Characteristically, however, Nixon turns this apparently inescapable humiliation into a political triumph as he successfully exhorts the masses before him to participate in a "drop your pants for America" campaign.

Whatever private fascination these scenes of subjugated but aggressive women and castrated but ultimately victorious, or at least unscathed, men may have for Coover, they seem peculiarly unenlightening when read in an age of feminine consciousness and sexual liberation. People reading Coover's works today are led to believe that the opportunities for women to express themselves sexually are limited to two. If the women in *The Origin of the Brunists, The Universal Baseball Association, Inc., J. Henry Waugh, Prop., The Public Burning,* and whenever they appear in *Pricksongs and Descants* are not aggressively appreciative sexual objects to be plied, plumbed, and plugged by insensitive men, they are castrators. Coover's men, on the other hand, are mostly insecure macho monsters whose fear of female rejection or their own inability to perform sexually leads them to use and abuse women for the gratification of their delicate but considerably inflated egos. With the exception of "The Brother" in *Pricksongs and Descants,* nowhere in Coover's fiction is there room for healthy sexual relationships. Inevitably, sex is associated with pain, humiliation, mud, and excrement. As a result, Coover's characters are prohibited from experiencing precisely what his fiction-making theory is supposed to afford: development. Reduced to stereotypes, they serve not to enlighten but to discredit whatever Coover holds up for ridicule.

The one exception to Coover's stereotypical treatment of his novels' characters, of course, is Richard Nixon, to whose public life the author has attached his fictional concerns. In other words, the major differences between the only fully realized character in all of Coover's novels and the protagonists that precede him are those presumed qualities that people have traditionally associated with the real-life former President. What is remarkable about *The Public Burning,* however, are the ways in which Coover is able to meld his fictional interests with the public figure with whom his readers are familiar. For example, Nixon, Tiger Miller of *The Origin of the Brunists,* and J. Henry Waugh, the creator of the Universal Baseball Association, Inc., are all interested in games. Games are, in Coover's words, what keep Miller and Henry going, but unlike Nixon, who tries to learn from what he observes in the world, they underestimate the value that people attach to game playing.

Nixon not only knows that games are "the very pulse and purpose of the nation" (*PB,* p. 89), he has learned how to play some of them. Relying on the living model, Nixon, then, Coover has been able to incorporate some of his fictional concerns into a character of the same name whose personality extends beyond the limited dimensions of protagonists such as Tiger Miller and J. Henry Waugh.

Another example of Coover's ability to incorporate his fictional interests with a protagonist whose complex personality and autonomy resist being reduced to a stereotype is Nixon's fascination with numbers. Like Ralph Himbaugh, the numerologist in *The Origin of the Brunists,* and J. Henry Waugh, Nixon creates numerological patterns from the incidents in his life, but, unlike these caricatures, he is not simple-minded. He knows from experience that the coincidences recorded by numbers can never amount to anything significant.

Nixon's preoccupation with games and numbers, however, like that of Coover's other protagonists, reveals his thinly veiled desperation to make some kind of sense out of the chaos he encounters daily. Throughout the story, he tries to convince himself he is playing an important role in an historical play that has been written for him by Uncle Sam. When he involves himself in the Rosenberg case, however, Nixon becomes inundated with ambiguities that he can neither decipher nor control. Frustrated, he expresses a theme that is at the center of all Coover's works: "There were no scripts, no necessary patterns, no final scenes, there was just *action,* and then *more action! . . .* It was what Uncle Sam had been trying to tell me: *act—act in the living present"* (*PB,* p. 362). And act he does. Though self-servingly motivated, Nixon travels to Sing Sing prison to extract a confession from Ethel Rosenberg, thereby saving her from the electric chair, obtaining information for Uncle Sam that he can use in his war against the Phantom, gaining approval from his constituents for his charity and diplomacy, and perhaps securing from the convicted spy some of the physical affection that is lacking in his relationship with Pat. Of course, he fails and becomes even more dependent on Uncle Sam to fulfill his need for order in the world. Lonely, paranoid, and pathetically opportunistic, the Vice President becomes "ready at last to do what I had never done before" (*PB,* p. 534). Hoping desperately for the presidency that will give him the power to control the chaotic flux in his life, Nixon allows the Incarnation of America to sodomize him as he confesses: "I . . . I love you, Uncle Sam" (*PB,* p. 534).

In addition to presenting its multi-dimensional protagonist, *The Public Burning* contains developments of narrative techniques that first appeared in earlier works. The most obvious of these is the remarkable intermingling of reality and illusion that most readers believed he had mastered in *The Origin of the Brunists* and *The Universal Baseball Association, Inc., J. Henry Waugh, Prop.* In *The Public Burning,* however, Coover develops further his process of blending fact with fantasy by making what the reader knows is fiction seem credible. Some notion of Coover's ability may be conveyed in a fictional conversation between Richard Nixon and Ethel Rosenberg in which the Vice President tries to convince the convicted spy that she does not love her husband:

"It's all been just an act, Ethel, and you know it! Part of the strategy!"

What . . . what are you saying—!"

"Who do you think you're fooling? You even forgot your anniversary last year!"

She was trembling. I was towering over her. "You're . . . you're saying this to divide us! It's not enough we have to die—"

"Admit it, Ethel! You've dreamed of love all your life! You dream of it now! I know, because I dream of it, too! But you've never known it, you've never given yourself to him, you've never given yourself to anybody!" My God! I was amazing.

"I . . . I don't believe in bourgeois romance," she said hoarsely, but there was no conviction in it. "That kind of love is sick, it's selfish, we mustn't—"

"Damn it, you know better than that! You're an artist, Ethel, a poet! You know what love is, what it might be! All the rest is just lies!"

Her resistance crumbled. I was amazed to watch it. She turned away, lowering her head. Almost inaudibly, she whispered: "I respect him so . . ."

"Yes, and you needed him, I know that—when you met him you felt abused and alone, and he was kind and sympathetic. I know all this, all about the illnesses and bad luck. I know about the bastard who tried to force himself on you, know how your own family frustrated your best hopes, how they failed to understand you, and then the Depression— what a lousy future you had to look forward to! And you thought Julie could save you from it, you thought—do you know what you thought back then?"

"Please . . . stop . . ."

"You thought he could save you from a meaningless martyrdom!"

She let out a soft anguished cry. I thought she would fall. I gripped her shoulders, turned her to face me. "We've both been victims of the same lie, Ethel! There *is* no purpose, there *are* no causes, all that's just stuff we make up to hold the goddamn world together—all we've really got is what we have right here and now: being alive! *Don't throw it away, Ethel!" (PB, pp. 435–36)*

Though not nearly so moving as this exchange between Richard Nixon and Ethel Rosenberg but interesting in their own right are the uses Coover makes of musical forms. As he did in *The Origin of the Brunists, The Universal Baseball Association, Inc., J. Henry Waugh, Prop.,* and "Morris in Chains," Coover writes folksongs that he incorporates into *The Public Burning's* narrative. In addition, these songs offer a comment on the insufferably folksy rednecks that sing them. The most offensive of these songs tells through the metaphor of a "groun'-hog hunt" a story about Uncle Sam and Joe McCarthy searching for agents of the Phantom. Coover's use of music does not end with folksongs, however, as they did in his previous works. In addition to "Human Dignity Is Not for Sale: A Last Act Sing Sing Opera by Julius and Ethel Rosenberg," Coover transforms a *Time* magazine review of President Eisenhower's favorite movie, *High Noon*, into an arrangement for Dimitri Tiomkin's theme song for the film.

> throughout the action dimitri tiomkin's
> plaintive high noon ballad sounds
> a recurring note of impending doo-oom
>   as the heat and drama
>   mount relentlessly
> to the crisi-hiss of high noon. . . . (*PB*, p. 237)

The song goes on to comment on the American idea of what it meant to be "a man" shortly after World War II, but it also serves as an ironic prelude to President Eisenhower's announcement that he will not grant clemency to the Rosenbergs. Like Gary Cooper, the hero of *High Noon*, President Eisenhower knows he "must be brave," as the words to Tiomkin's song tell him, and face the Phantom, "a man who hates me," or "lie a coward in my grave" (*PB*, p. 241). "At the focus of pressure," records America's laureate balladeer, *Time*, "Dwight Eisenhower did not flinch . . ." (*PB*, p. 244).

In *The Origin of the Brunists,* Coover uses America's dependence on television to comment on the popular culture's view of reality. As the Brunists march toward the Mount of Redemption, Elaine Collins tells her boyfriend that she wishes she could go home and watch the end of the world on television, as if whatever occurs there is more real. In *The Public Burning,* Coover makes a similar but more powerful statement as he records the reaction of several children to the electrocution of Julius Rosenberg. Fascinated by the first two jolts, they are bored by the third and want to go home and watch Mickey Mouse. On their television sets at home, however, the story of the Rosenbergs has already been incorporated into the medium's most popular situation comedies. On the then-popular "Jack Benny Show," Coover creates a situation in which Jack needs a costume to wear to a pie-crust contest that Betty Crocker is holding prior to the Rosenbergs' executions. The prize is $1,000. Willing to make a small investment in a costume that may bring a larger return, Jack asks Rochester to offer a dime to a passing panhandler for the use of his coat. True to form, Jack promises to return the coat after the contest providing the bum gives back Jack's dime.

Not to be outdone by Jack Benny, ventriloquist Edgar Bergen tries to convince his puppet, Charlie McCarthy, that the state's electric chairs can be counted on to do their job.

Charlie: Say Bergen . . . ?
Bergen: Yes, Charlie?
Charlie: That chair works by electricity, doesn't it?
Bergen: Yes.
Charlie: Well, what happens if it doesn't kill 'em? They're only singers, you know, not conductors. . . . (*PB*, p. 451)

The performers who come closest to stealing the show, however, are the Marx Brothers. Speaking of Ethel Rosenberg, Groucho says,

. . . she's a mighty lak' a rose!
Chico: Oh, a Pinko, eh? We're gettin to da bottom a dis!
Groucho: You been there, too, hunh?
Chico: She'sa da one what's stole-a da bum, eh?
Groucho: She didn't steal it, she was born with it!
Chico: And she gave it to the Russians?
Groucho: She gave it to everybody! (*PB*, p. 455)

As ironically funny and satirically revealing of the American character and human nature as they may be, these seasoned entertainers are amateurs when compared with Richard Nixon, who, unexpectedly caught on the stage in Times Square with his pants down, tells the American people:

I want to make my position perfectly clear! We have nothing to hide! . . . I say it is time for a new sense of dedication in this country! I ask for your support in helping to develop the national spirit, the faith that we need in order to meet our responsibilities in the world! It is a great goal! And to achieve it, I am asking everyone tonight to step forward— right now!—and drop his pants for America! (PB, pp. 481-82)

Brilliantly reconstructing the voices of real characters into fictional ones, Coover shows how the evident villains of America's past, Nixon, Cohn, McCarthy, Eisenhower, and the rest, as bad as they were, are only the manifestations of the evil that lies at the core of American sensibilities. Whether on radio or television, in the movies or Times Square, at home or abroad, Americans seem beset with an aimless determination to do anything, even drop their pants, to assert their power and avoid seeing themselves as they really are. Tragically, Americans seem to need people like Nixon to channel their desires of the moment. When these desires backfire, they look for scapegoats, like Julius and Ethel Rosenberg.

One other inventive technique, which Coover uses as a metaphor of the existential man caught in the chaotic flux of his environment, is the wanderer. Unlike the wanderers in *Pricksongs and Descants* who choose to alienate themselves from society, the wanderer in *The Public Burning* is similar to Sycamore Flynn of *The Universal Baseball Association, Inc., J. Henry Waugh, Prop.* Trying to make sense out of a situation with which he is familiar but does not fully understand, Flynn unsuccessfully tries to find a way out of the fiction that Henry has created for him. Similarly, the man in *The Public Burning* that leaves a showing of *House of Wax* wearing his cardboard 3-D glasses gets caught up in the horrifying revelry of Times Square and wants out. Seeing the world from the new perspective that his glasses provide, he is frightened by the images that closely resemble those of the horror movie in which innocent people are murdered and eventually go up in flames. Like Sycamore Flynn, who cannot find his way out of the ballpark, and many of the Universal Baseball Association's other players, the man wonders if the world may be turned by some malevolent design.

As remarkable as this and other developments from techniques introduced in previous stories are, however, their cumulative effect in *The Public Burning* often seems long-winded and inadequately substantive. Because the position Coover takes in his novel is one of angry but simple satire, even his vast powers of invention cannot sustain the narrow range of surface emotions that the novel stimulates. Had Coover skimmed over his unenlightening comments about injustice and mass insanity and concentrated instead on less crude versions of the Rosenbergs' case, the role Nixon played in America's Early Warning Sentinel

System, and the American composite in Uncle Sam, he might have written a better novel. As a guideline for improving *The Public Burning,* he might have consulted his review of Louis Nizer's *The Implosion Conspiracy,* which seems to contain many of the same shortcomings as Coover's novel. Addressing Nizer's honesty as a writer, Coover suggests that the lawyer/author

might have provided us, given his special knowledge and even admitting his biases, with new insights into the Rosenberg case. . . . He might . . . have examined the controversial evidence (was the Gold hotel registration card an F.B.I. forgery? were the bomb sketches worthless? what evidence did the prosecution suppress to tighten its case?) . . . he might at least have asked how fair play is possible when the prosecution has so much more rehearsal time and knows what the script is going to be, while the defense has to play it as improvisation theater, not even sure what props are going to be used or where they are coming from. . . . Did the Rosenbergs bring into that 1951 courtroom the hint of a life style that somehow threatened all those middleclass accountants and public servants? Was the cause for their suspicious courtroom behavior in fact their pretending to be somebody they were not during the trial? Nizer does not have room in his spy drama and love story for these questions.[9]

Unfortunately, Coover could not find room in his satire, either, and what might have been is yet to come. As it is, *The Public Burning* pillages history for material that Coover can process into show-off exercises that call attention mostly to the narrative designs of their author. Clever, witty, inventive, and as ambitious as *The Public Burning* may be, however, its limited emotional range and excessive concern with constructs hamper Coover and his readers like a pair of dropped pants.

III   *From Politics to Pornography*

"The Cat in the Hat for President," a spoof on the hoopla that attends the way Americans choose their national leaders, and "Whatever Happened to Gloomy Gus of the Chicago Bears," which introduces a "completely metaphor-free" character that clearly resembles Richard Nixon, are two novella-length works for which Coover interrupted his writing of *The Public Burning.* Nevertheless, the author's role in these works is similar to the one he has played in all of his preceding fictions: "The role of the author, the fiction maker, the mythologizer, is to be the creative spark in the process of renewal; he is the one who tears apart the old story, speaks the unspeakable, makes the ground shake, then shuffles the bits back together into a new story. Partly anarchial, in other words, partly creative—or re-creative. The organizers of society—the politicians, chiefs, bureaucrats—will go ahead and rebuild the thing from time to time, but that's not what the storytellers are doing. . . . I enjoy the fun of stirring things up, breaking the rules, punching holes in the structures so as to see through to the mysteries—even if only to rediscover what it was you liked about society when it was still all of a piece. The artist's role, then, is priestly in a way; he's there, at his best, as a voice of disturbance" (Woolf, p. 54).

Representing the organizers of society in "The Cat in the Hat for President" is the novella's narrator, Mr. Brown, whose "life in business and politics has been long, successful, and colorless" (*CH*, p. 9).[10] Ironically, however, many of Mr. Brown's attitudes are similar to those of Coover and the anarchial protagonists of his other fictions. Like Tiger Miller of *The Origin of the Brunists* and the Universal Baseball Association's J. Henry Waugh, for example, Brown believes in the fictional nature of the reality man has created: " 'Liberal,' 'conservative,' 'left,' 'right,' these are mere fictions of the press, metaphoric conventions to which politicians sooner or later adapt" (*CH*, p. 9). Similarly, Brown is as interested in games as Miller, Waugh, and Coover, but he plays them with the tenacity of *The Public Burning*'s Richard Nixon: "Rationally, I accept the idea that life is at best a game, yet my nature is serious and fiercely competitive: I fight to win and couldn't help it if I would" (*CH*, p. 11). Nevertheless, Brown "needed the familiar as much as anyone else and so found comfort in the traditional" (*CH*, p. 34). His belief that "revolt derring-do, mess-making are not my way. I liked my mother" (*CH*, p. 23) may well serve as a response to Coover's suggestion that an entropic society periodically necessitates its artists doing "everything that has been taboo: wear women's clothes, kill the sacred animal and eat it, screw your mother, etc." (Gado, p. 157). Unfortunately for Brown, however, his constituents and political colleagues are tired of the familiar: "We are weary of war, weary of the misery under our supposed prosperity, weary of dullness and routine, weary of all the old ideas, weary of all the masks we wear, the roles we play, the foolish games we sustain" (*CH*, p. 20).

Attempting to free Brown and those who share his point of view from the illusions of order that their fear of reality has produced is the Cat in the Hat, a character from Dr. Seuss's children's stories, who, says Coover in another context, "makes us think about all the things we shouldn't do, all the impossible, apocalyptic things, and weakens and tears down structure so that they can be rebuilt, releasing new energies" (Gado, p. 157). Brown sees the Cat and his antics, which seem better suited for a circus than a political convention, as inherently destructive, "but what" he rationalizes, "is destroyed except nay-saying itself, authority, social habit, the law of the mother, who, through violence in the name of love, keeps order in this world, this household" (*CH*, p. 23). Eventually, Brown, who is the chairman of the challenging political party, capitulates to the enthusiastic response the Cat's unorthodox approach to politics has created and agrees to support his candidacy for the Presidency.

On the day of his nomination, however, the Cat appears on the convention floor wearing a pair of roller skates and holding up a cake on a rake. On top of the cake is a goat balancing an umbrella on his nose, and on top of the umbrella wobbles a fishbowl with a protesting fish inside. Soon the whole assemblage falls and the entire hall is engulfed in water from the fishbowl. The fish, which is now of Leviathan size, swallows up all the delegates and then spews them forth into a glass-encased arena that happens to be the fishbowl on top of the umbrella that is being balanced by the goat who is standing on top of the cake that the Cat in the Hat is balancing on his rake. "Now you can see/What I can do!" announces the party's nominee, "I can give you/Something new!/Something true/And impromptu!/I can give you/A new view!" (*CH*, p. 26).

Although Brown can appreciate the liberating perspectives offered to him and the party's delegates by the Cat in the Hat, he suspects the Cat might be a greater threat to the status quo than a new metaphor for appreciating the old ways. His friend Clark, however, comforts him with the thought that "any great liberation is always accompanied by a vague sense of loss. . . . What we must do, Mr. Brown," says Clark, echoing Coover in his prologue to *Pricksongs and Descants*, "is help all men once more to experience reality concretely, fully, wholly, without mystification, free from mirages, unencumbered by pseudo-systems" (*CH*, p. 27).

The Cat, however, soon proves to be every bit as tireless, astounding, unpredictable, and unmanageable as any of Coover's fictions. Whether popping out sewers in Hyannis, bathing in the Chicago River, juggling live bears in Yellowstone, swishing eight-foot-long rubbery clubs at skittery golf balls with eyes and noses and making holes in one, flying on top of a cross-eyed, baldheaded eagle that clutches a popgun and a jar of olives in its claws and shits on the opposing party's nominee, or exposing the absurdity of America's normalcy by bouncing out of every television set in the nation and dragging with him spies, cowboys, comics, pitchmen, sobsisters, cops, preachers, aviators, gumshoes, crooners, talking animals, quarterbacks, panelists, and more, the Cat's message is the same: "We've been living in a shutdown world. We're opening it up. It's worth it" (*CH*, p. 36).

As valuable as the Cat's alternatives to conventions may be, however, they are resisted by educators, labor leaders, businessmen, minority groups, priests, poets, bureaucrats, warriors, journalists, and others who have located for themselves a verity in the traditional. Responding to the threat of a military takeover, the Cat's campaign managers set him up to be skinned alive by a mob of status-quo maintainers. What follows the cat's death is an orgy that echoes those of *The Origin of the Brunists, The Universal Baseball Association, Inc., J. Henry Waugh, Prop.,* and *The Public Burning:* "While the Cat burned, the throng fucked in a great conglobation of races, sexes, ages, and convictions; it was the Great American Dream in oily actuality, and magically, every time an orifice was newly probed, it uttered the *Me-You!* Cat-Call" (*CH*, p. 43).

In addition to the apocalyptic orgy, which tears down many of America's conventional structures in order that they can be rebuilt by the establishment, "The Cat in the Hat for President" contains a share of the folksongs and vaudeville routines that are familiar to Coover's readers. Two of the Cat's campaign enthusiasts, Joe and Ned, dressed like their candidate in striped hats, bow ties, and gloves, shuffle a soft shoe to their "Cat in the Hat Campaign Song."

Following the song, Joe and Ned pass out buttons, introduce

the Cat-Call (*Me-You!*), and laugh their way through the worst vaudeville gags this side of "McDuff on the Mound":

Ned: Say, Mr. Joe, our nation has got *cat* problems!

Joe: How do you mean, *cat* problems, Mr. Ned? Can you make me a list?

Ned: Make you a *list?* Why, Mr. Joe, I'll make you a *catty*-log! . . . I mean, things is catty-clysmic, Mr. Joe. They are catty-plectic, catty-strophic, and all cattywomptious! (*CH*, p. 13).

Unlike the routines that wasted time on the basepaths of Coover's other fictions, however, the gags in "The Cat in the Hat for President" comment on the infantile sensibilities apparent in the kinds of campaigns and images to which Americans respond. Similarly, Coover's story can be read not only as another appeal for his readers' acceptance of numerous narrative and imaginative possibilities, but also as a metaphor for the tolerance of extremities that can separate people from the "human constant," and "carry us out to something new where these old ways of identifying ourselves will seem sad and empty" (*CH*, p. 36).

"Whatever Happened to Gloomy Gus of the Chicago Bears," the second novella for which Coover interrupted his work on the Rosenbergs, tells the story of a machinelike creature who bears an obvious resemblance to the Richard Nixon of *The Public Burning*. Like the protagonist of *The Public Burning* and those of other Coover works, "winning was everything for Gloomy Gus. . . . In a magazine interview, he once said: 'I have never had much sympathy for the point of view, "it isn't whether you win or lose that counts, but how you play the game." One must put top consideration on the will, the desire, and the determination to win'" (*GG*, p. 64). Similarly, both Nixon and Gloomy Gus are debaters, actors, pianists, playwrights, and expert potato mashers for their moms. Both have a keenly developed sense of paranoia, rely more on discipline than intelligence, and are attracted to Jewish women. Unlike the Nixon of *The Public Burning*, however, Gloomy Gus is more of a caricature than a person: "Gus not only lacked political awareness, he lacked awareness of any kind. He had no core at all. It was this nothingness at the center that we all settled on as the essential Gloomy Gus" (*GG*, pp. 50–51).

As might be expected, Coover portrays his protagonist through a variety of songs and vaudeville techniques. When some Socialist friends catch Gus coupling with his girlfriend, Golda, he responds by standing at attention and singing "The International." When one of these Socialists hears that Gus has been killed during a strike by some local factory workers, he begins to compose a song about the fallen footballer. Because Gus had no interest in the factory or the dispute between its owners and their workers, the song gives the novella's narrator, Meyer, the opportunity to speak at length on Coover's familiar theme about the dangers that lay in mythifying real events into history.

Coover's most amusing vaudeville routine, however, occurs whenever Gus hears the number "twenty-nine." According to his brother, Gus was such a stupid athlete, he could never remember his quarterback's count and was continually penalized for illegal procedure. Consequently, Gus's coach gave his halfback a single number by which he could set his plays in motion. Because Coover's simple-minded clown cannot distinguish between on and off the field, however, his reaction to "twenty-nine" is always the same. At one point in the story, Gus interrupts a conversation, in which a group of people are trying to determine the year of America's great stock-market crash, by running through a stove that, fortunately for him, is not lit at the time. Gus offers the same response to Golda when she tells him her age.

And what is the moral contained in Coover's adaptation of an old Abbot and Costello routine? Simply this: that people like Gloomy Gus and Richard Nixon, who replace compassion with the discipline necessary to achieve money, power, and fame, become little more than coldhearted clowns. Ironically, Gus, perhaps like Nixon, needs most what he works hardest to separate himself from. As Golda says, when she hears her lover has been shot after running through a confrontation between police and striking union workers as if they were opponents on the gridiron, "Perhaps, if we had only given him more love and understanding, this woulda never happened . . ." (*GG*, p. 105).

To give his important but simplistic comment on what counts most in life a credible context, Coover places it against a backdrop that includes the Duke of Windsor's wedding, the Spanish Civil War, the extermination of the Jews in Germany, and the struggle between labor and management in America.

Unfortunately, what little Coover has to say about these matters, namely, that lack of love and understanding is what caused them and, in the immediate everyday world, they counted for little more than the White Sox's league standings, is blurred by the slapstick surface action of the events in Gloomy Gus's life. Furthermore, when the clown's adventures are read in light of some of his creator's more humanly perceptive or technically inventive works, "Whatever Happened to Gloomy Gus of the Chicago Bears" does not mark a significant achievement for a man of Coover's talent. In fact, what Coover has to say about the pornographic films he saw in *Suck* magazine's First Annual Wet Dream Festival may apply to his novella: "There's not much in the stuff, ten or fifteen minutes of it is a very long time indeed. If porno-festivals are to thrive and take over the world, they'll probably have to learn something . . . about pace and timing, honesty and awe, complexity and self-criticism. They will have to be taken out of the hands of bagmen and randy innocents and given over to filmmakers, environmental artmakers, metaphysicians, and musicians. Rite of passage will have to be distinguished from holy farce, . . . clergy and congregation alike led away from the temptation of the simplistic and regressive."[12]

As pornography, "Lucky Pierre and the Cunt Auction" and "Lucky Pierre and the Music Lesson" may be two of Coover's most purely entertaining stories. The first of these narratives opens with Lucky Pierre at an auction barn. While the auctioneer conducts the bidding on old pornographic films, seven-inch vinyl latex penises, and the like, Coover's "hero" inspects the cunts that await their turn on the auction block.

Eventually one of the cunts he examines pleases him: "96. CUNT, VICTORIAN—*Guar't'd Upper Class, Antique Husb, Believed Imp't't. No Other Owners, Genuine Guilt Feelings, Note esp. Full Heav'g Br'sts Tipt with Deliciously Small Nipls of that Fine Pink Color w'ch so Strongly Denotes Virg'y in the Poss'sor.*"[13] Obsessed by his desire to possess the cunt, Lucky Pierre enters into a bidding war unethically managed by the auctioneer, who fleeces the bidder of much more money than the sexual object is apparently worth. Feeling much like the protagonist of Coover's "The fallguy's faith," for whom the gesture is as important as the act, Pierre leaves the auction barn with the laughter of bidders ringing in his ears.

"Lucky Pierre and the Music Lesson," which carries one step

further Coover's attack on self-inflation and the treatment of people as objects, begins with a young girl's inability to please her music instructor, who punishes the girl by throwing her across his lap and beating her with a birch rod. With the help of several other pupils, who have also been beaten, the instructor removes the girl's underpants and arouses himself sexually by cutting ribbons of wealed flesh and blood into the girl's bottom. At this point in the story, a voiceover conversation comments on the scene Coover depicts. Soon the reader realizes that the music lesson is a movie with Lucky Pierre playing the role of the teacher. Lucky Pierre is also one of the people commenting on the film; the other is a woman porno star named Cissy, who recently purchased the vintage film at an auction. As the music lesson continues, Lucky Pierre and Cissy become sexually aroused by its events, which culminate with the instructor raping the young girl and eventually killing her. Nevertheless, whatever relief the reader may have experienced in learning that the music lesson is a movie vanishes when Pierre tells Cissy that the child in the film actually died while he was attacking her. Instead of being horrified by this revelation, however, Cissy applauds Pierre's dedication to his art: "You're a genius, Luke!" she says, "And, love, whose cock but yours could have pulled off that ending?"

As the movie reaches its conclusion, Pierre and Cissy talk about how the music lesson might appear if it were filmed at the time the story is taking place. Excited by the film and their conversation, they begin making love, the description of which verbally surpasses any of Coover's other orgies and leaves the reader with a music lesson he's not soon to forget: "She lifts one thigh to commence the main exposition, and he fingers her f-hole, sets her plectrum quivering, her valves hopping, her rosebud resonating. . . . Cissy frets with his capastato, while he blows a jubilant blast up her pipeworks: it sets her golden belly quavering, then comes rumbling brassily down her wind-way: *poop-titty-poop-poop-WAAAHH.*" [14]

CHAPTER 5

On Coover

COOVER'S FICTIONS clearly emphasize their author's interest in providing his readers with the kinds of metaphors that are necessary for a healthy imagination. Unfortunately, Coover says between the lines in every story he writes, people today have lost their desire for the thrill of discovery. They have become comfortable with having their conventional viewpoints confirmed through a limited range of artistic forms that have outlived their usefulness. Each of Coover's stories, then, invites its reader to relinquish one or more of his traditional approaches to art and participate with its author in an exercise of wit that frequently juxtaposes what is fantastic in life with the everyday.

The principal method through which Coover liberates readers from sensibilities that have been deadened by the familiar is irony. Irony enables Coover and his readers to distance themselves from traditional forms without isolating themselves from the human content of those forms. As a result, Coover's readers have the opportunity and pleasure of tearing down many of society's inherited approaches to art and life without losing their concern for humanity's condition. The result is a healthy sense of humor and the awareness of a developing consciousness.

In his first novel, *The Origin of the Brunists,* Coover presents his readers with a fascinating interplay of realistic and artificial modes that enable his readers to enjoy his mockery of traditional narrative forms while simultaneously employing its conventions in vitally new ways. Similarly, Coover undercuts man's dependency on religion and history while revitalizing his interest in fiction as a way of ordering his universe. *The Universal Baseball Association, Inc., J. Henry Waugh, Prop.,* like *The Origin of the Brunists,* is primarily concerned with man's need to create order through fiction: "You could say I wrote the baseball book not for baseball buffs or even for theologians but for other writers"

(Gado, p. 150). The fictions may be highly artificial, as in the case of games or mathematical formulas, or they may be more subjective, such as when they appear in the forms of myth, religion, and history. When man forgets his role as a creator of fiction, however, and begins to accept the works of his imagination as fact or truth, he finds himself imprisoned and manipulated by the very perspectives that he constructed.

In the twenty-one fictions collected in *Pricksongs and Descants,* Coover focuses his attention on reinterpreting familiar stories, which have been traditionally revered for the human truths they contain, and emphasizing the variety of technical and imaginative possibilities available when art and life are free from limiting conventions. The nature of reality, Coover seems to be saying, is so complex that any single way of interpreting it must necessarily be false. Hence, the problem of nature's multiplicity becomes its own solution. For art truly to represent nature, it must be as variable as nature itself.

Having recast the appeal for originality and multiplicity that unified *Pricksongs and Descants* into the four one-act plays that comprise *A Theological Position,* Coover returned to his interest in *The Public Burning,* a new view of the events surrounding the executions of Julius and Ethel Rosenberg that makes as legitimate a claim to truth as any objective statement of the facts:

The truth for a narrator is not the same as the truth for a journalist, historian, or scientist. The author's truth comes out of a set of metaphors—even if sometimes he gives them names and calls them characters. So that in a work of fiction you can have a sense of terrible truth about a thing that doesn't seem to relate at all to the so-called real world. Normally, though, the metaphors *will* relate to the real world—language itself, after all, is a product of that world—and so fiction will have a second standard of truth. That is, the metaphors themselves have in the first place some *need* to arise, and the word "truth" is probably as good as any to describe why this is so. (Woolf, p. 55)

Reworking history, as he has done with myths, legends, and fairy tales, may represent a new arena in which Coover can explore further the interests that have been of primary concern to him since *The Origin of the Brunists:* "Like in the creation of myths, I sometimes transpose events for the sake of a kind of inner coherence, and there's a certain amount of condensation and so on, but mainly I accept that what I'm dealing with here is a society that is fascinated with real data, facts and figures, dates, newspaper stuff. I can't mess around too much with the data here lest I lose contact with that fascination." Nevertheless, "my own inclination as a writer is to move more and more in that direction, condensing, moving facts around, juxtaposing living and dead persons, myth and history. That would seem a useful and proper way to write about the past" (Woolf, p. 55).

However Coover chooses to reinterpret history, his readers can be assured of accomplished and inventive stories that deal absurdly and metaphysically with the human condition without losing their sense of humor. In fact, what Coover has to say about Jose Doñoso's *The Obscene Bird of Night* may very well serve as an ideal for himself and his art:

His purpose here is not to clarify a point but to produce a miracle. This miracle takes many forms—some ironic, some awesome, some "real," some allegorical, some legendary—but the climactic miracle is a kind of hat trick. . . . The story line is like a great puzzle with everything in it from burlesque to romance, magic to murder, often bizarre, yet always invested with a vibrant, almost tangible reality. . . . Yes, a miracle, a climactic act of magic for a book that is itself both Miracle and Monster, like the best of this century's American fiction."[1]

Notes and References

Chapter One

The comments compiled in this chapter have been excerpted from interviews with Coover that were conducted over the course of his career to date by Leo Hertzel (*Critique* 2:3 [1969]: 25-29), Frank Gado (*First Person: Conversations on Writers and Writing.* [Schenectady, N.Y.: Union College Press, 1973], pp. 142-59), and Geoffrey Wolff ("An American Epic," *New Times* 19 August 1977, pp. 54-55). Sources are identified by author's name in the text.

1. Translated by Samuel Putnam for *The Portable Cervantes* (New York: Viking Press, 1951), p. 707.

2. William Gass, *Fiction and the Figures of Life* (New York: Alfred A. Knopf, 1970), p. 104.

3. *The Fabulators* (New York: Oxford Univ. Press, 1967), p. 41.

4. Prologue to "Seven Exemplary Fictions," *Pricksongs and Descants* (New York: E. P. Dutton & Co., Inc.). Page references in the text are to this edition, and are identified by *PD*.

5. Neil Schmitz, "Robert Coover and the Hazards of Metafiction," *Novel* 7 (Spring 1974): 210-19. Robert Scholes, "Metafiction," *Iowa Review* 1, (Fall 1970): 100-15.

6. Roger Shattuck, *The Banquet Years* (New York: Random House, 1968), p. 328.

7. Neil Schmitz, "Robert Coover and the Hazards of Metafiction," p. 213.

8. *Iowa Review* 1:4 (1970). Subsequent page references in the text are to this edition.

9. Larry [Lawrence] McCaffery. "The Reliance of Man on Fiction-Making: A Study of the Works of Robert Coover" (Dissertation Abstracts International 36, 2810A) p. 145.

10. *Fiction and the Figures of Life*, p. 272.

11. "The Last Quixote: Marginal Notes on the Gospel According to Samuel Beckett," *New American Review* 11 (New York: Simon and Schuster, 1971), p. 143.

12. "One Summer in Spain," *Fiddlehead*. Autumn 1960, p. 18.

13. *Evergreen Review* 25 (July-August 1962): 96.

Chapter Two

1. *"The Origin of the Brunists,"* [review], *Book Week,* 9 October 1966, p. 14.

2. *"The Origin of the Brunists,"* 1 November 1966, p. 279.

3. "Real Life in an Unreal World," *Saturday Review,* 15 October 1966, p. 38.

4. *The Origin of the Brunists* (New York: G. P. Putnam's Sons, 1966). Page references in the text are to this edition and are identified by *OB.*

5. "All the Hidden Nuts Cracked Open," *New York Times Book Review.* 25 September 1966, p. 4.

6. "Imaginary Borges and His Books," *Fiction and the Figures of Life,* p. 126.

7. From the Preface to *The Water Pourer* (Bloomfield Hills, Mich.: Bruccoli Clark, 1972). Page references identified in the text by *WP.*)

8. *The Universal Baseball Association, Inc., J. Henry Waugh, Prop.* (New York: Random House, 1968). Page references in the text are to this edition and are identified by *UBA.*

9. "Robert Coover's Fictions," *Iowa Review* 2-3 (Fall 1971): 105.

10. *Antaeus* 24 (1977): 111-12.

11. "Robert Coover's Fictions," p. 108.

12. "What's Wrong with the Christians," *Critique 11:3 (1969): 22.*

13. "Humor and Balance in Coover's *The Universal Baseball Association, Inc.,"* *Critique* 17:1 (August 1975): 89.

14. "The Man behind the Catcher's Mask: A Closer Look at Robert Coover's Universal Baseball Association," *University of Denver Quarterly* 12:1 (1968): 173-74.

15. "Robert Coover's Fictions, p. 10.

16. "The Dice of God: Einstein, Heisenberg, and Robert Coover," *Novel* 10 (Fall 1976): 58.

17. "McDuff on the Mound," *Iowa Review* 2 (Fall 1971). Page references in text identified by *MM.*

Chapter Three

1. The handful of stories of which Coover speaks are collected within *Pricksongs and Descants* under two titles: "Seven Exemplary Fictions" and "The Sentient Lens." These stories were published before Coover's first novel, *The Origin of the Brunists* (1966) and are discussed in the second chapter of this book.

2. Some of the more important stories that Coover decided not to include in *Pricksongs and Descants* include "Blackdamp," *Noble Savage,* 4 October 1961; "The Square Shooter and the Saint," *Evergreen Review* 25 (July-August 1962); "Dinner with the King of

England," *Evergreen Review* 27 (November–December 1962); "D.D., Baby," *Cavalier* (July 1963); "The Second Son," *Evergreen Review* 31 (October–November 1963); "The Neighbors," *Argosy* (London: January 1965); "The Mex Would Arrive in Gentry's Junction at 12:10," *Evergreen Review* 47 (June 1967); "The Cat in the Hat for President," *New American Review* 4 (August 1968).

3. *Fiction and the Figures of Life*, p. 105.

4. *Pricksongs and Descants* (New York: E. P. Dutton & Co., Inc., 1969). Page references in the text are identified by *PD*.

5. *Fiction and the Figures of Life*, p. 106.

6. *Novel* 7 (Spring 1974): 214.

7. "The Dead Queen," *Quarterly Review of Literature* 8: 3–4 (1973): 304. Further page references in text.

8. "Some Notes About Puff," *Iowa Review* 1:1 (Winter 1970): 29, 31.

9. Robert Coover, "Valley of the Fallen, 3 July" from "One Summer in Spain," *Fiddlehead*, Autumn 1960, p. 15.

10. "Robert Coover and the Hazards of Metafiction," p. 24.

11. *Harper's*, January 1972, p. 82.

12. *Fiction and the Figures of Life*, pp. 106–107.

Chapter Four

1. *Evergreen Review* 47 (June 1967): 63–65, 98–102.

2. *A Theological Position* (New York: E. P. Dutton & Co., Inc., 1972). Page references in the text are to this edition and are identified by *TP*.

3. Neil Schmitz, "A Prisoner of Words," *Partisan Review* p. 134.

4. 8 August 1977.

5. "The Public Bungling," *Texas Monthly*, August 1977, p. 162.

6. *Commentary*, October 1977, p. 68.

7. "Real People, Mythic History," *New York Times Book Review*, 14 August 1977, p. 26.

8. *The Public Burning* (New York: A Richard Seaver Book/The Viking Press, 1977). Page references in the text are identified by *PB*.

9. *New York Times Book Review*, 11 February 1973, p. 4.

10. *New American Review* 4 (1968). Page references in the text are identified by *CH*.

11. *New American Review* 22 (1975). Page references in the text are identified by *GG*.

12. "The First Annual Congress of the High Church of Hard Core (Notes from the Underground)," *Evergreen Review* 89 (May 1971): 16, 74.

13. "Lucky Pierre and the Cunt Auction," *Antaeus*, Spring–Summer 1974, pp. 156–57.

14. "Lucky Pierre and the Music Lesson," *New American Review* 14 (1972): 208, 211.

Chapter Five

1. *New York Times Book Review*, 17 June 1973, pp. 1–2.

Selected Bibliography

PRIMARY SOURCES

1. Novels
The Origin of the Brunists. New York: G. P. Putnam's Sons, 1966;
London: Barker, 1967.
The Public Burning. New York: A Richard Seaver Book/The Viking
Press, 1977.
The Universal Baseball Association, Inc., J. Henry Waugh, Prop. New
York: Random House, 1968; London: Hart-Davis, 1970.

2. Collected Short Stories
Pricksongs and Descants. New York: E. P. Dutton & Co., Inc., 1969;
London: Cape, 1971.

3. Uncollected Short Stories
"Beginnings," *Harper's,* January 1972, pp. 82–87.
"Blackdamp," *Noble Savage* 4 (October 1961): 218–29.
"The Convention," *Panache,* 1977.
"The Cat in the Hat for President," *New American Review* 4. New
York: New American Library, 1968, pp. 7–45.
"D.D., Baby," *Cavalier,* July 1967, pp. 53–56, 93.
"The Dead Queen," *Quarterly Review of Literature* 8 (1973): 304–13.
"Debris," *Panache,* 1971.
"Dinner with the King of England," *Evergreen Review* 27 (November–December 1962): 110–18.
"Encounter," *Panache,* 1971.
"The fallguy's faith," *TriQuarterly* 35 (Winter 1976): 79–80.
"Lucky Pierre and the Cunt Auction," *Antaeus,* Spring–Summer 1974,
pp. 13–14.
"Lucky Pierre and the Music Lesson," *New American Review* 14. New
York: Simon and Schuster, 1972, pp. 201–12.
"McDuff on the Mound," *Iowa Review* 2 (Fall 1971): 111–20.
"The Mex Would Arrive at Gentry's Junction at 12:10," *Evergreen
Review* 47 (June 1967): 63–65, 98–102.
"The Neighbors," *Argosy,* London (January 1965).
"The Reunion," *Iowa Review* 1 (Fall 1970): 64–69.

149

"The Second Son," *Evergreen Review* 27 (October–November 1963):
    72–88.
"Some Notes About Puff," *Iowa Review* 1 (Winter 1970): 29–31.
"The Square Shooter and the Saint," *Evergreen Review* 25 (July–
    August 1962): 92–101.
"The Tinkerer," *Antaeus* 24 (1977): 111–12.
The Water Pourer. Bloomfield Hills, Mich.: Bruccoli Clark, Inc., 1972.
"Whatever Happened to Gloomy Gus of the Chicago Bears?" *New
    American Review* 22 (1975): 31–111.

4. Poems
"Letter from Patmos," *Quartery Review of Literature* 16 (1969):
    29–31.
"One Summer in Spain: Five Poems," *Fiddlehead.* Canada (Autumn
    1960): 13–14.

5. Collected Plays
A Theological Position. New York: E. P. Dutton & Co., Inc., 1972.

6. Translations
"The Osprey and the Sparrowhawk," "El gavilan y el quebran-
    tehuesos" by Ricardo Estrada. *Quarterly Review of Literature*
    15:3–4 (1968). p. 259–61.

7. Reviews and Essays
"The First Annual Congress of the High Church of Hard Core (Notes
    from the Underground)," *Evergreen Review* 89 (May 1971):
    201–12.
"The Gossip on the Wall," a review of *In Evil Hour* by Gabriel Garcia
    Marquez. *New York Times Book Review,* 11 November 1979, pp. 3,
    30.
"The Implosion Conspiracy" by Louis Nizer. *New York Times Book
    Review,* 11 February 1973, pp. 4–5.
"The Last Quixote," *New American Review* 11. New York: Simon and
    Schuster, 1971, pp. 132–43.
"The Master's Voice," *New American Review,* pp. 361–88.
"The Obscene Bird of Night" by Jose Doñoso. *New York Times Book
    Review,* 17 June 1973, pp. 1–2.

8. Film
On a Confrontation in Iowa City, written, directed, and produced by
    Coover at the University of Iowa in 1969.

SECONDARY SOURCES

1. Interviews with Robert Coover

GADO, FRANK. *First Person: Conversations on Writers and Writing.* New York: Union College Press, 1973, pp. 142-59.

HERTZEL, LEO J. "An Interview with Robert Coover," *Critique* 11:3 (1969): 25-29.

KADRAGIC, ALMA. "An Interview with Robert Coover," *Shanti,* Summer 1972, pp. 57-60.

WOOLF, GEOFFREY. "An American Epic," *New Times,* 19 August 1977, pp. 54-55.

2. Criticisms of Coover's Works

COPE, JACKSON I. "Robert Coover's Fictions," *Iowa Review* 2 (1971): 94-110. Cope discusses the artist's loss of self through the act of imaginative projection and Coover's unremitting interest in "the teasingly predictable forms of number and measure."

HECKARD, MARGARET. "Robert Coover, Metafiction and Freedom," *Twentieth Century Literature* 22 (1976): 221-27. Heckard places Coover's works within the context of metafiction, that is, works which "share a renunciation of content, a tendency toward formalism, a lack of suppositions about human nature, and preference of method to metaphysics."

MCCAFFERY, LARRY [LAWRENCE]. "Robert Coover" in *Dictionary of Literary Biography, Volume Two: American Novelists since World War II,* eds. Jeffrey Helterman and Richard Layman. Detroit: Bruccoli Clark/Gale Research, 1978, pp. 106-21. Based on McCaffery's unpublished Ph.D. dissertation, "The Reliance of Man on Fiction-Making: A Study of the Works of Robert Coover" (*Dissertation Abstracts International* 36, 2810A, 1975), which analyzes in detail *The Origin of the Brunists, The Universal Baseball Association, Pricksongs and Descants,* and *A Theological Position* as they present Coover's theme of man's need to order his world through fictional constructs. "In desire for stability and final truths, however, man dogmatically asserts fictions that he claims owe their existence to the world and not his own ideology."

SCHMITZ, NEIL. "Robert Coover and the Hazards of Metafiction," *Novel* 7 (Spring 1974): 210-19. What is exhibited in metafiction is a mental procedure that takes in its own processes as well as the object of those processes. Cooooer's metafiction fails as literature because it is "nothing but a mode: a series of acrobatic exercises in technique." Furthermore, Coover's concentration of effect "only mirrors the superficiality of this genre."

SCHOLES, ROBERT. "Metafiction," *Iowa Review* 1 (Fall 1970): 100-15.

Coover's technique in *Pricksongs and Descants* "is to take the motifs of folk literature and explode them into motivations and revelations, as the energy might be released from a packed atomic structure." When extended, Coover's fiction apparently either lapses into a more fundamental mode of fiction or risks losing all fictional interest in order to maintain its intellectual perspectives."

3. Reviews

The Origin of the Brunists

CAPOYA, EMILE. "Real Life in an Unreal World," *Saturday Review*, 15 October 1966, pp. 39-40. "Gifted as well as ambitious, . . . Mr. Coover has attempted to revive the naturalistic novel for serious literary purposes by grafting onto it fantastic, surreal, and hysterical elements."

SCHOTT, WEBSTER. "All the Hidden Nuts Cracked Open," *New York Times Book Review*, 25 September 1966, p. 4. "En route to his final formalization of the Brunists, . . . Mr. Coover takes apart the economy, power structure, social order and sexual codes of a small town gone berserk with holiness. . . . It is a novel of intensity and conviction." Coover "may become heir to Dreiser or Lewis."

Pricksongs and Descants

GASS, WILLIAM. "Pricksongs and Descants," *Fiction and Figures of Life* (New York: Alfred A. Knopf, Inc., 1971, pp. 104-109. Gass discusses *Pricksongs and Descants* as a construct: "Sharply drawn and brightly painted paragraphs are arranged like pasteboards in ascending scales of alternating colors to compose the story, and the impression that we might scoop them all up and reshuffle, altering not the elements but the order or rules of play, is deliberate."

MAHIN, LINDA RUTH. "Experiments in Fiction: Poetic Visions of Samuel Beckett, Jorge Luis Borges, and Robert Coover," *Dissertation Abstracts International* 37, 298A, 1976. Mahin examines Coover's contention that "all crucial beliefs are mythic in nature, but we should examine our myths in order to make sure they are still useful. Myths that use up their utility should be abandoned and new ones created, always aware that they are a fictional view of reality. Role of the artist is to create new fictional forms out of mythic residues of the unconscious and offer them as patterns of experience."

OATES, JOYCE CAROL. *"Pricksongs and Descants," Southern Review* (Winter 1971): 305-306. "Coover . . . exists blatantly and brilliantly in his fiction as an authorial consciousness, not at all interested in creating old-fashioned worlds for us to believe in, but interested—obsessed, rather—in creating a dimension of personality that is pure style, pure eloquence, 'form' equalling 'content.'"

WESTERVELT, LINDA ALLYNE. "The Role of the Reader in Modern Anatomy: A Study of the Fiction of John Barth, Robert Coover, and Thomas Pynchon," *Dissertation Abstracts International* 37, 2188A, 1976. Westervelt develops Coover's partly ironic attitude toward his characters. The author "is skeptical of the systems his characters invent and believe in." Coover's plan is to lead the reader toward an identification with the characters, frustrate him, and teach him through irony and parody the danger of believing in fiction as reality. Westervelt concludes tht people who create formulas to explain their existence risk enslavement to their creations.

The Public Burning
EDWARDS, THOMAS. "Real People, Mythic History," *New York Times Book Review*, 14 August 1977, pp. 8-9. Coover reconstructs history into fiction in order to comment on society. "Villains of the past . . . aren't the source of evil but its agents, dupes, or victims; the evil is us, the aimless determination of a people to be up and doing something—anything—to assert our power rather than to have to know too clearly what we are and why. We need our Nixons, Coover seems to say, both because they cater to our most reckless desires of the moment and because they are so easy and gratifying to punish afterwards."
WOOLF, GEOFFREY. "An American Epic," *New Times* 9 (19 August 1977): 49-57. Coover's novel "exploits historical data from a period just now passing—the cold war—to postulate a comical and awful mythology about the nature of celebration, institutionalism, community, love, ambition, pain and energy in American life. . . . The book's effect is anarchic, subversive of public order and decency; it libels half the country, and scandalizes the rest."

A Theological Position
AARON, JULES. *"The Kid,"* *Educational Theatre Journal*, October 1975, pp. 419-20. Aaron points out how Coover's play satirizes "America's need for a bandit 'hero' as well as our desire for the security of living life like a 'B' movie with a 'happy ending.' Beneath the facade of the play's metaphoric saloon is the tough core of the self-destructive American Way of Life."

The Universal Baseball Association, Inc., J. Henry Waugh, Prop.
HANSEN, ARLEN. "The Dice of God: Einstein, Heisenberg, and Robert Coover," *Novel* 10 (Fall 1976): 49-58. Hansen explains Coover's fascination with name and myth, which, when "applied to the substance of reality effect an expression of pattern and meaning, . . . an undertaking that atomic physicists can well appreciate."
KERRANE, KEVIN. *"The Universal Baseball Association, Inc.,"* *Journal of*

Popular Culture 8 (Fall 1974): 441-87. Coover's mythic and symbolic premise allows him to indulge in playful theological speculation (J. H. Waugh=Jahweh; the UBA=the universe), but his real subject is the creative imagination. The novel doubles back upon itself, inviting us to contemplate the novelist's own relationship to his characters, and his God-like ability to make life out of the raw material of mere language."

SHELTON, FRANK. "Humor and Balance in Coover's Universal Baseball Association, Inc.," *Critique* 17:1 (August 1975): 78-90. Shelton explains how the folk concerns in Coover's novel "coexist with the most sophisticated speculation on the nature and meaning of history, myth, and religion. Thus, the novel provides two perspectives on reality, the folk or country perspective of most of the ballplayers and the sophisticated urban perspective of Henry Waugh and Coover himself. . . . .

Index

Barth, John, 15, 17, 30
Beckett, Samuel, 29, 31; *Malone*, 29
Borges, J.L., 17
Bultmann, Rudolf, 19

Cervantes Saavedra, Miguel de, 15; "Two
    Exemplary Fictions," 15–16
Coover, Robert, on his use of irony, 19;
    on his attraction to religion, 18–19;
    on the nightmare quality of contem-
    porary fiction, 35–36, 102; on the
    tones he adopts towards his subjects,
    66–67; on the structures he employs,
    69–70, 79–80; on the role of the
    fiction-maker, 70, 80–81, 81–82, 101,
    108–109, 133–34, 142–43.

WORKS:
"A Pedestrian Accident," 101–103
"A Theological Position," 114–16
A Theological Position, 108–17, 125,
    142
"Barcelona Air Terminal, 28 May," 32
"Beginnings," 98–99
"Blackdamp," 40, 78
"Dinner With the King of England,"
    36–39, 58, 77–78
"In a Train Station," 23, 27–28, 43
"Incidents in the Streets of the City,"
    103–105
"J's Marriage," 18, 20–22, 61
"Klee Dead," 23, 28–30, 31, 43, 47,
    96
"Love Scene," 112–13
"Lucky Pierre and the Cunt Auction,"
    139
"Lucky Pierre and the Music Les-
    son," 139–40
"McDuff on the Mound," 74–78
"Morris in Chains," 92–93, 111, 129
"Panel Game," 23–25, 60, 65, 76, 79

Pricksongs and Descants, 15–30,
    79–107, 116, 126, 127, 132, 135,
    142
"Quenby and Ola, Swede and Carl,"
    89–92, 93
"Rip Awake," 113–14
"Romance of the Thin Man and the
    Fat Lady," 93–96, 102, 113
"Scene for 'Winter,' " 31–32
"Seven Exemplary Fictions," 15–30,
    76, 80
"Some Notes on Puff," 87, 88–89
"The Babysitter," 103–105
"The Brother," 18, 19–23, 61, 127
"The Cat in the Hat for President,"
    117, 133–37
"The Dead Queen," 87–88
"The Duel," 109–11
"The Door," 82–84, 85, 86–87, 91
"The Elevator," 99–101, 113
"the fallguy's faith," 139
"The First Annual Congress of the
    High Church of Hard Core," 139
"The Gingerbread House," 84–87,
    89, 91, 93
"The Hat Act," 105–107
"The Implosion Conspiracy," 133
"The Kid," 109, 111–12
"The Last Quixote: Marginal Notes on
    the Gospel According to Samuel
    Beckett," 16
"The Leper's Helix," 31, 34–35
"The Magic Poker," 96–98, 99, 107
"The Marker," 23, 25–26, 79
"The Mex Would Arrive in Gentry's
    Junction at 12:10," 109
"The Milkmaid of Samaniego," 31,
    32–34
"The Obscene Bird of Night," 143
The Origin of the Brunists, 40–57, 60,
    61, 64–65, 69, 72, 78, 80, 111, 116,

155

125–26, 127, 128, 129, 130, 134, 136, 141
The Public Burning, 117–33, 136, 137, 142
"The Reunion," 18, 19, 22
"The Second Son," 58–60, 78
"The Sentient Lens," 16–17, 30–36
"The Square Shooter and the Saint," 36–39, 58, 77–78
"The Tinkerer," 67–68
The Universal Baseball Association, Inc., J. Henry Waugh, Prop., 40, 57–74, 75, 77–78, 81, 102, 111, 114, 116, 126, 127, 128, 129, 132, 134, 136, 141
"The Valley of the Fallen, 3 July," 87, 89
The Water-Pourer, 56–57
"The Wayfarer," 23, 26–27
"Whatever Happened to Gloomy Gus of the Chicago Bears?" 133, 137–39

Defoe, Daniel, 34

Fiedler, Leslie, 42

Ionesco, Eugene, 110; *The Killer,* 110

James, Henry, 20

Joyce, James, 20
Jaspers, Karl, 19

Mailer, Norman, 42
Murdoch, Iris, 15

Nabokov, Vladimir, 17
Nizer, Louis, 133; *The Implosion Conspiracy,* 133

Pynchon, Thomas, 17, 30

Robbe–Grillet, Alain, 41

Salinger, J.D., 37; *Catcher in the Rye,* 37
Scholes, Robert, 15, 17
Shattuck, Roger, 17
Sontag, Susan, 42

Tiomkin, Dimitri, 130
Twain, Mark, 21, 36; *The Adventures of Huckleberry Finn,* 36; *Letters from the Earth,* 21

Vonnegut, Kurt, 15

Whitman, Walt, 93